Money and Me

A Woman's Guide to Financial Confidence

Cynthia G. Yates

VINE
BOOKS

SERVANT PUBLICATIONS
ANN ARBOR, MICHIGAN

Vine Books is an imprint of Servant Publications especially designed to serve evangelical Christians.

The names and circumstances in this book are drawn from many women the author has met at retreats and seminars. All have pseudonyms and are fictional composites. Any similarities between the names and characterizations of these individuals and real people is unintended and purely coincidental.

This book is designed to provide accurate information in regard to the subject matter. It is sold with the understanding that the author and publisher are not rendering legal, financial, or other professional services.

Published by Servant Publications
P.O. Box 8617
Ann Arbor, Michigan 48107

99 00 01 02 10 9 8 7 6 5 4 3 2 1

Printed in the United States of America
ISBN 1-56955-072-7

LIBRARY OF CONGRESS CATALOGING-IN-PUBLICATION DATA

Yates, Cynthia, G. 1947–
Money and me : a woman's guide to financial confidence / Cynthia G. Yates.
   p.   cm. — (Women of confidence series)
Includes bibliographical references and index.
ISBN 1-56955-072-7 (alk. paper)
1. Finance, Personal.   2. Women—Finance, Personal.   I. Title.   II. Series.
HG179.Y365   1999
332.024'042—dc21   98-51435
                                                          CIP

To my mother,
and others like her,
who struggled to survive.

Contents

Acknowledgments

Seven professionals offered critical evaluation of this manuscript. I wish to thank them for their good counsel, their willing spirits, and their servant hearts:

Muffie Thomson,
Vice President & Manager, Flathead Bank of Lakeside

Randall A. Snyder,
Snyder Law Office

Jean M. Parson,
CFP

Mary "Molly" Soper Yates,
LCSW

Cherie Toole Hansen,
Re/Max Realty

David Finkel,
CPA

Kris Wade,
Inventory Control Manager, Greentree Financial

Special Thanks

to each woman who responded to my survey and shared insight for Women*Speak,* and to Liz Heaney, my editor, for the excellent help in crafting this book.

Introduction

My Own Journey Toward Financial Security

When I was young, I wrote poetry. Life seemed uncertain and turbulent. Security was illusive, impossible, the stuff of dreams, and I hid my fears in page after page of rhythm and rhyme.

My life as a child was happy some of the time. My younger sisters and I had a mother who went to great lengths to make it so. My father, though I adored him, was ill-suited to bear responsibility for anyone but himself, and seemed to have trouble at that. My memory is vivid of Mom dumping out her purse, searching through coat pockets, and emptying piggy banks for gasoline and ice cream money. Sunday afternoons were spent exploring nearby towns and neighborhoods, and capped by a visit to relatives (often in time for dinner!). Attempts at savings were thwarted by Dad's need for new suits, or nights on the town, as one savings plan after another was depleted and we were left behind. My sisters and I lay in bed upstairs listening and scared, as arguments over money prevailed. I picked wildflowers and peddled them to neighbors. "Here is money for our Sunday ride," I would say.

Being a teen in a house without plenty didn't bother me much. Arguments continued, and my mother still worked hard. I remember watching her lone silhouette come closer and closer toward our home on dark, snowy nights, as she pushed her way through drifts in the field, toward the little light in our upstairs window. The bus stop was so far away. I always switched the light on for her, something she might not know to this day.

I worked hard during high school years, and money went straight to my mother—with some left for me to spend on others. Money made it possible for me to buy friendship and affection.

Upon graduation, I got a job. College would only interfere with earning and contributing. Besides, my meager college savings had been spent long ago. Armed with a fifty-two-week-a-year weekly paycheck, I continued to spend money on others, and lived from moment to moment. My survive-the-day mentality stuck with me like some kind of superglue. I earned, I spent. And so it went. The concept of money *management* or savings never entered my mind. Many a time my roommate and I searched our purses and coat pockets to find change for a raid on the all-night deli.

I chased illusion right into marriage, and wed a man with no capacity to manage money. We finagled finances for seven years before our house of cards fell down. We made money, we spent money. We never saved. When mismanagement and deceit caught up with us, he was gone, everything was lost, and our young son depended solely upon me.

"Down-and-out" translated to "homeless and penniless," and in a short time, I was filled with terror. The financial burdens of single-parenting brought me to the brink of despair. With purse and pockets long empty, illusion could not carry me a step further. I had reached bottom and found it dark and slippery-sided. Climbing out would take work, for sure, but it would also take thought. For the first time, I began to break destructive patterns (make/spend/survive) as I started the long and rewarding trek out of that pit. Foothold by foothold, I stepped tentatively toward the future, away from just surviving for the day.

Today those days seem a long way off. My little boy is married and in graduate school; I rest comfortably in the arms of a strong and sensible husband; debt no longer terrorizes me. What's more, the savings begun in mid-life continue to grow. I've learned many important lessons and skills through the years, lessons that prepared me for the future and taught me to look to my Lord. Alongside my husband, I've charted a path toward financial security, and put my trust in God. I no longer compensate for feelings of inadequacy by spending; my friends are genuine, and not bought; and my impulse buying is under control (and I still write poetry).

I also write books. My purpose with *Money and Me* is to provide a guidebook to caution, cajole, and cheer on other women as they journey toward financial responsibility. I want this book to be a road map, sometimes offering more than one route to a destination, which I have charted through training, experience, and from wandering down a few dead-end streets myself!

To make this book different, and not simply the next in a long line of books on how to manage money, or a rehash of advice you could get from a supermarket newsstand, I decided to include three things that would make this book fun, yet practical.

1. Tea *Time!* These sections are interactive questions, or information, to make you think, confront your circumstances, communicate, learn, or *do* something that will help you to hone your money management skills.

2. Women*Speak*. Each chapter begins with the voices of other women who offer their wisdom, foibles, and experiences in the area of money. There is something comforting when someone speaks your language, even if it's the language of "been there, done that."

3. At the end of each chapter, I've included two simple reality checks: *Where I Am Now* and *Where I'd Like to Be*. The purpose of this section is to encourage you to think about your situation as it pertains to the chapter you've just read. It is my conviction that "half the work is in the starting." In other words, by thinking about your situation and *writing down* your thoughts, you are well on your way to defining and fulfilling your goals.

I did my utmost to make this book comprehensive. I even stepped into "forbidden" territory and devoted part of a chapter to point a scolding finger at consumer glut, and I included specific counsel on tithing.

Please read this book with a pencil or pen in hand. If the pages end up dogeared, underlined, highlighted, and a smudgy mess, I will know I did my job well!

And now I wish *you* well, and extend my hand in friendship, as I invite you to join me on a path that leads to freedom from financial bondage and from worry about tomorrow.

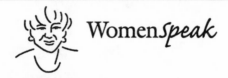 Women *speak*

"How I wish that I knew when I was young what I know now about money management."

———

"I was married to a man who never asked where I spent the money he gave me, or why I needed what I purchased. He just handed me a wad of bills when I asked for money. When he died, I had a rude awakening. I had to tighten my belt and learn how to budget for myself. The funds I was left with, and the small Social Security checks I received, couldn't possibly last as long as I hoped to live. So now I live on a budget, and have to do without many things I'd love to participate in, like joining my friends on trips, or seeing shows."

———

"My husband and I are able to manage money cooperatively because we are partners in all aspects of our lives, and we discuss and agree on our expenditures before we make them."

———

"I worry about money all the time. I can't help it. It's like I live in fear."

———

"It seems like every time I turn around, I'm turning over a new leaf, always determined to buckle down and get serious about budgeting, and stuff like that. I'm good for a while, and then I slip right back into old patterns—destructive patterns. And what's worse, when I'm out of control I know it, and I don't care."

one

What Mama Never Taught Us About Money

"Stop at the bank. I want to see how much money I have."

I pursed my lips and turned the car toward my mother's bank. My fingers drummed the steering wheel as I waited while she went inside to check her account balance. There I sat, publisher of a newsletter on money management, author of a book on frugal living, popular speaker on women's finances, and my mother refuses to balance her checkbook. Her reason? "I made a mistake in math once, so now I trust the bank. They don't make mistakes."

Oh, brother.

This from the woman who single-handedly reared three girls, got two of them through college, and worked right up to age sixty-five. This is a woman who had to scrimp and save and juggle finances just to exist—a strong woman, a survivor—and she wouldn't, or couldn't, balance her checkbook. She grew up in the Depression, endured a horrific marriage, played brilliant bridge every Tuesday afternoon, and she didn't have a clue about how much money she had in the bank.

Without the benefit of a small pension and Social Security, my mother would be penniless. How could this be?

I've run into many women like my mother, and not all of them in their eighties. Young women, old women, single women, married women, widows. Rich or poor, they have all had their turn at bat. I've heard from them in group discussions, in whispered phone conversations, and as they sob. Most women, it seems, though concerned about financial security, automatically disqualify themselves from such things as investing, or manipulating funds toward definitive goals.

Money management, to some, means nothing more than paying the bills on time. Part of this is cultural. There seems to be a stigma, or taboo, attached to money management and financial planning. It's been a man's game, at least in perception. Women, in the meantime, accomplish Herculean feats in childrearing and home management. They run businesses; run countries; fly into space; turn three simple staples, from almost bare cupboards, into Epicurean delight; but they can't (or won't) reconcile their bank statements. In other words, many women are capable of *making* money, but they fall short when it comes to *managing* money.

This contradiction is more common than you would think. For instance, it might surprise you (especially if you read the introduction to this book) to know that during my young adult years, as a highly motivated and well-trained representative for a large firm, I sold employee benefit programs, pension plans, retirement plans, and insurance. I marched confidently into homes and businesses, and rattled away with my speech: "The future is coming; you must plan for it today."

"Accidents do happen," I implored young couples. "You must protect yourself from the unexpected today."

"People do die," I told employee groups with passion. "You must insure financial liquidity today."

Was I being hypocritical? No! I meant what I said, and can happily say I played a part in helping others become financially secure, over time. I, on the other hand, was caught in destructive behavior (which became destructive behavior squared when my first husband entered the picture), and I never actualized my predicament. I was the proclaimed professional. It was my job to counsel people to manage money wisely. My business card said so! Yet my own affairs were in shambles. A case of "the shoemaker's children going barefoot"? Believe me, there are a lot of us padding around in old, tattered house slippers. Take Jan's story:

Jan struck me as a "nineties" kind of woman. Everything about her told me she was on top of her world. She listened attentively to the money management talk I was giving, and then followed me to the parking lot. There she leaned against her car and wept heavy tears. Jan, a single parent due to divorce, was seconds away from losing her house and car; her children were taxing her paycheck beyond belief; she was about to be delinquent with her credit card bill (which was maxed); and nobody, not even her closest friends or family, had a clue. Jan is a certified public accountant.

There are other women like Jan, many who offer pretense and bluff, who are staggering under crushing debt and fear. There are women who spend money out of control, hoping for temporary release from anxiety or despair—shopping as therapy, shopping as addiction. There are women who struggle to live within their means, and don their Wonder Woman cape daily, determined to create a happy haven for their children and mates. And there are women who choose to remain ignorant of family affairs, or who are left in the dark by their husbands who avoid all talk of financial matters. Almost all manage to hide their fears and insecurities behind Sunday smiles.

I am reminded of an elderly widow at a retreat. The lady was filled with dignity, and bore herself with a warm but confident manner. If ever there was a woman who "had it all together," it was she. Yet when I challenged the women in the church to write a paragraph describing their financial predicament, that woman, like Jan the accountant, wept heavy tears.

Or take Gladys' situation. "Write a prayer to God about your finances," I coached the crowd of women. We were in the last stretch of a two-day seminar on frugal living. I watched as each woman wrote long and thoughtfully. On impulse, I asked them to share their feelings. The catch was, they could only use one word. These women knew each other well; some were best friends, yet new, strange words came from their mouths: *rage, hope, resolve, anxiety, blessing, sorrow.* And then we came to Gladys.

Gladys can best be defined as a "typical church lady." I would bet that Gladys always brings a delicious casserole to potluck suppers, and helps do the dishes. She probably knits mittens for the needy, helps to clean the church, and prays for your very soul. That day Gladys admitted that she was scared. Heads whipped to attention, and eyebrows scrunched on foreheads as people in the room wondered if they had heard right. *Gladys? Scared?* What was going on? Gladys chose to speak.

"My husband's Social Security doesn't cover our expenses. So every month I go to the bank and borrow more money on our credit card, and I'm scared."

I've run into many, many women like Gladys over the years.

What's Going On?

Everything is in a state of change. Things are not the same. Here's a very simple rundown of what has happened: As the twentieth century picked up momentum, advances in technology beckoned people off the farm and into urban settings to work in factories. America was growing and profitable. Industry created jobs. Jobs meant homes and cars, and every new gadget to come our way. Loyalty was high, as employer and employee alike entered into a lifelong commitment honored by productive work and good retirement.

Not long ago—close enough for some of us to remember—people saved money and paid cash for nearly every purchase except their home, and mortgages were written in accordance with retirement goals.

Not only was financial security more certain, but the fabric of family was, for the most part, different. (There were glaring exceptions to this generality, as in my circumstance.) Family once meant father, mother, and children, accompanied by uncles, aunts, grandparents, in-laws, cousins, nieces, and nephews. Kitchen tables buckled under Sunday afternoon feasts, as voices filled the air around the dining table with familiar sounds. Holidays were no less crowded, as children did their best to behave, and everyone got along relatively well. People—neighbors as well as relatives—were there for each other.

School was a place of safety, even though dress codes or uniforms brought out rebellion in the best of us, as we tried to hike a skirt an extra inch or roll a shirt sleeve in defiance. If we were careful, we didn't smash our lunch before noon, and if we were really lucky, the brown bag our mom had filled that morning had a goodie stashed inside. The only dilemma facing us was choosing between white and chocolate milk. After school, most of us went home to mom. Usually, on a bus or a bike.

Murder and robbery happened someplace else, like in big cities. And in big cities, we knew criminal activity was happening on the "other side of the tracks." Charlatans and hucksters were around, but they didn't abound. Elder abuse through fraud was real, but rare.

Sounds somewhat mythical, doesn't it? To some, it is. Yet facts prevail; things were different not so long ago, before the cultural authority of American beliefs, ideals, and traditions began to dissolve.

In the past thirty-plus years, structures and traditions have been overthrown. Some of the change came from impatience over important issues: racial bigotry, urban poverty, environmental disregard. Some of it came from outright rebellion, as the counterculture announced its arrival with a scream, bringing along with it expectations for personal fulfillment that can now be considered unrealistic. Whether you agree with the new perspective or not—and unless you've been counting penguins in the Antarctic for nearly four decades—everything has changed.

How Have Things Changed? Let Me Count the Ways

Because of even more advances in technology, because we are leaving the Industrial Age and charging full-floppy-disk into the

Information Age, because of trade agreements with less-developed countries, and because of corporate downsizing, the security of a lifetime job at the brick factory—or any factory—is nonexistent. Modernity has driven us apart and lashed out at loyalty as one of its first casualties. People aren't there for each other anymore.

Inflation and recession, and then inflation again, have clobbered the dollar into submission, as it shrinks to a shadow of its former robust self. Mom has to find a way to help; clipping coupons and scouring thrift stores isn't enough anymore.

Families are fractured and far away. Many men, now liberated from traditional morality by the sexual revolution, have abdicated their roles as providers and co-regents in their homes. Holidays are often meaningless hurry-up affairs, with presents piled high, maybe in an attempt to mollify the hunger in our hearts for stability and security.

Peer pressure at school goes beyond the absolute necessity of wearing the right clothes. Now the pressure is to participate in dangerous and immoral behavior.

Crime has jumped the tracks and mainstreamed into daily life. Not only do many people fear physical harm or loss, but sophisticated scams and fraud are rampant, targeting the elderly, and women, in particular.

Smack in the middle of all of this change came easy credit, knockin' at our front door. "Buy now, pay later" became the theme song of excited consumers who could have just about anything their hearts desired, without sacrifice or second thought. Instant gratification fit nicely with grand plans for personal fulfillment. We were on a roll. Credit, designed to stimulate industry, became industry. Credit now drives our economy.

Nearly everything in our budget can be purchased with credit. Enter credit abuse.

According to a booklet called *Out of Hock*, nearly 110 million Americans have 950 million credit cards—almost nine per person![1]

The apostle Paul wrote to Timothy: "For the love of money is a root of all kinds of evil" (1 Tm 6:10). Was he ever right! We could add to that: "The misuse of money is the cause of many heartaches."

What Does This Have to Do With Balancing Our Checkbooks?

Plenty. Whether it is right or not—whether we like it or not—the future is not secure. There is no longer absolute moral (or religious) authority that guarantees the certainty of lifelong marital commitment. Government programs such as Social Security are said to be on shaky ground, and private businesses (along with private pension plans) file insolvency regularly. In the midst of this comes woman, clutching "rights-talk" to her bosom, as she marches aggressively from favored (albeit restricted) status into the fray. We are all affected.

It is time to become savvy about personal and family finances. No matter who you are, no matter what your circumstance, no matter what your age, not only do you need to plan for tomorrow, you must be a wise and faithful steward of God's provision today.

Proverbs 6:6-8 says: "Go to the ant, you sluggard, consider its ways and be wise! It has no commander, no overseer or ruler, yet it stores its provisions in summer and gathers its food at harvest." While this proverb deals primarily with the sluggard, or lazy person, it makes an important point: One of the tiniest of God's creation knows times and seasons and is able to accumulate enough food to last through the winter. The lazy person discovers too late that winter and hunger are here. May I paraphrase? Ants not only work hard, they *manage* their resources.

Proverbs 31:10-31, a favorite passage of mine, describes a virtuous woman, and gives us a glimpse of her inexhaustible potential. Clothed with strength, honor, and gentleness, the biblical woman:

- has noble character (verse 10)
- has a husband who is fully confident in her (verse 11)
- is able to select quality merchandise (verse 13)
- is able to find and wisely purchase food (verse 14)
- is able to make wise investments (verse 16)
- works diligently (plans) (verse 17)
- is profitable in trading (verse 18)
- opens her arms to the poor (verse 20)
- outfits herself and her household well (verse 22)
- is very industrious and good in business (verse 24)
- *can laugh at the days to come* (verse 25)

It is incumbent upon us to become Proverbs 31 women, knowledgeable about budgets, investments, and consumer purchase. We must break loose of complacency, fear, denial, or survival mode. In plain English, we may feel as if we are crashing into an all-male domain, as we get out of the bleachers and step up to the plate, but it's time to play a little ball. If all we continue to do is duck and dodge hard balls, sooner or later we're going to get popped in the nose.

On the other hand, divorce in America seems to be running a dead heat with marriage. Sadly, divorce does destroy Christian homes, as well. The result of divorce is tragic beyond measure. Not only do we suffer profound social disruption and destruction, but—since this book is about financial matters—women, in particular, are left holding the proverbial bag, and it's often empty. "We want justice!" we yell with our fists clenched, as we hold up our banner for equal rights. Huh? The equality some of us have campaigned for is about as balanced as last month's bank statement.

Much of the burden of family finances, motivation, and nurturing has shifted to women, and until the right balance can be achieved—until men are able to grasp the urgency for them to regain and earn their place as coleaders in their homes, with all the attendant responsibility that comes with that distinction—women had better learn skills at money management.

Another factor in this equation is mortality. The simple, irrefutable fact is that woman outlives man. Sooner or later, she's going to have to look finances square in the eye.

Let's put it another way. If you are married to a responsible and loving husband who

- provides for you and your family, and pays the bills;
- considers you co-regent of financial matters, and keeps you informed;
- has made provision for both of you, should one get sick or have an accident;
- has diligently planned for retirement;
- is neither a tightfisted grump nor a spendthrift;

- understands the biblical imperative to tithe and share and care;
- will never die and leave you widowed . . .

put this book down and go read a novel.

How nice it would be if we didn't have to bother with all of this! Many of us (myself included) would rather someone else bear the responsibility of balancing the checkbook we are so skilled at using! Besides, to some, money management seems rather bothersome—a necessary evil.

The Love of Money

Money is neither good nor bad. Dollar bills and coins, certificates of deposit, and stocks and bonds happen to be the currency we use for trade. In this book, we will regard money as a tool, and nothing more. We will learn how to properly use that tool and care for it so it will not rust or rot in our care, and we will find ways to use our tool to build hope for others.

The purpose of this book is to empower you, beginning with your attitude, to approach money management enthusiastically, and to be prepared, as the woman in Proverbs, for any cold weather that might come your way. Hand in hand we will explore principles of working, saving, carefully using money, and of sharing with others. We will never, ever, let money or financial security become the overriding focus of our attention, or our trust; all the money in the world will not replace the security we find in God alone.

If you are a woman who wants to become a better steward of your financial resources, this book is for you. If you already are a master at money management and have developed the attitude, knowledge, and skills to budget, invest, and share, this book will serve as a reference, a refresher, and an "atta-gal!"

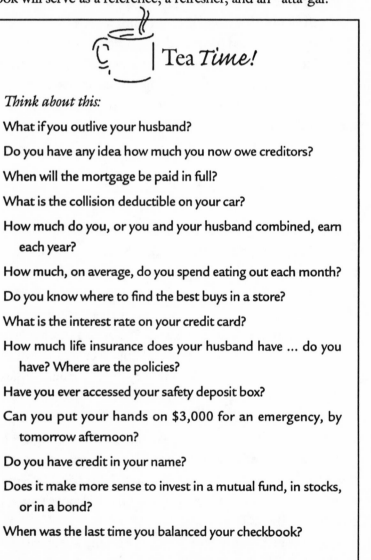

Tea *Time!*

Think about this:

What if you outlive your husband?

Do you have any idea how much you now owe creditors?

When will the mortgage be paid in full?

What is the collision deductible on your car?

How much do you, or you and your husband combined, earn each year?

How much, on average, do you spend eating out each month?

Do you know where to find the best buys in a store?

What is the interest rate on your credit card?

How much life insurance does your husband have ... do you have? Where are the policies?

Have you ever accessed your safety deposit box?

Can you put your hands on $3,000 for an emergency, by tomorrow afternoon?

Do you have credit in your name?

Does it make more sense to invest in a mutual fund, in stocks, or in a bond?

When was the last time you balanced your checkbook?

Money and Thee: Finding Your Way

If you had trouble answering the above questions, you need this book! But don't be overwhelmed. We're going to get through this together. Whether your fear is tiny, or as big as the sky, there is nothing you can't handle through God's abundant providence. He might not send the award squad to your door, but he will send his grace. Let God the Holy Spirit empower you and guide you. If you are determined to become a financially secure woman, then roll up your sleeves and put on your baseball cleats—we've got work to do.

In chapter two, we will begin to look at your financial condition. My hope is that when you have applied the principles of this book, you will be able to smack a home run over the fence, and never again strike out when hard balls come your way. From this moment on, you will start your run for home base, toward becoming a financially secure woman.

Now it's your turn to write. Think about what you have read in this chapter. How does it apply to you? Soul-search a little, and jot down your thoughts.

Where I am now: _____

_____

_____

Where I'd like to be: _____

_____

_____

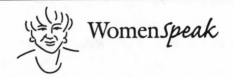 Women*Speak*

"I've made so many mistakes, I don't know where to start. I guess among the biggest was ignoring my gut feelings about the money I spent. I got into credit card debt, had a negative balance in the checking account, and unpaid bills, all because I didn't listen to that gut feeling of 'You are overspending again!' The feeling of walking out of a store knowing I had overspent was unexplainable. As I'd get into my car, I'd feel that quivery feeling—probably the same feeling a skydiver feels before jumping out of a plane. Yep, the my-checkbook-just-took-a-dive feeling, with nothing to catch it when it fell."

———

"The smartest thing a woman can do to protect herself financially? Be more involved with family finances, including mortgages, investments, and bills."

———

"My secret for living within my means is knowing that God has never let me go without the things I need. I know that God rewards us for spending money wisely. When I have faith in God, my needs are always met. The most important thing I have learned, when dealing with money and possessions, is that God cannot change your circumstances until you are content within them. That doesn't mean just sit back and accept your life for what it is, and desire no more. It means, be happy with what God has given you, and you'll see new opportunities and gifts beyond what you ever wanted."

———

"My husband will not take my fears seriously. I don't know if we will ever get out of our mess."

two

Taking Control of Your Purse Strings

As Christians, our primary stewardship responsibility is to reach others with the Good News, and to live for the glory of God. That responsibility includes wise use of the gifts God has bestowed upon us. *It also includes our outward attitude and Christian witness, as we manage financial affairs.* For instance, have you ever considered that you bring God glory when you pay your bills on time, spend wisely, prepare for the unexpected, plan for your future, tithe, and help others?

In their book called *Smart Money,* Jerry and Ramona Tuma and Tim LaHaye ask: How can we effectively witness to non-Christians if they see no difference between our lives and theirs? If they don't see peace, freedom, love, and joy in our lives, what will draw them to Jesus?[1]

When we also remember that God owns everything, the matter of caring for his possessions—stewardship—takes on new meaning. But God isn't a grumpy old tightwad! His Word provides us with guidance for successful living. The Bible is filled with the story of redemption, but it is also filled with admonition and instruction. If we are faithful to Scripture, God will be faithful and true, and help us as we muddle through daily affairs. When we take the Bible's counsel, we will be in right relationship with the owner of all things. Caring for his possessions will be a joy. If we understand from the start that we are administrators of God's provision, we will become more responsible and accountable for what he's entrusted to us.

In order to responsibly handle the finances God has given you, you'll need to define your financial circumstances, muster the courage to look at poor habits or destructive behavior, and then chart a financial plan that will certainly bring rewards, not the least of which will be peace in your heart, and weight off your shoulders.

Where Are You?

A motorist stopped at a Maine farmhouse to ask directions. "Can you tell me how to get to such and such a place?" she inquired. The farmer, with dry humor typical of that region, responded, "You cain't get they-ah from he-ah." You can't get where you are going unless you know where you are.

Let's put it this way: Suppose you had a pain in your toe. Would your doctor automatically prop your toe on her desk and slice it open, or cut it off? No! She'd find out everything she could about your toe—and your behavior—and diagnose your condition first. Your shoe might be too tight. You might have bumped your toe on the nightstand. You might be developing arthritis.

No matter what your financial concern or predicament, you will never, ever, be able to establish a strategy toward any goal unless you first know exactly where you are. You will never, ever, be able to overcome destructive habits unless you know exactly what got you into a mess in the first place.

Debt and Denial

Some of us are scared witless to face our financial predicament. (One of the surest ways to know you're doing a swan dive smack into the never-ending pit of debt is refusal to open your mail.) It's called denial. By hiding from the truth (or in the case of unopened mail, hiding the truth), we don't have to face the failure, the pain, or the raw terror of the mess we're in. We sink deeper and deeper into despair as we deny the reality of the situation, as if not facing the problem will make it go away.

Denial dances hand in hand with other behavior. One friend, for instance, refuses to think about her husband ever dying, and will have no part of sensible planning or preparation; she will not allow the mention of such things. "I don't want to deal with it!" she barks. If she outlives her husband (as statistics predict), she will have plenty to deal with.

Others live for the moment and can't be bothered with concern for tomorrow, not realizing that "the moment" is the tomorrow of yesterday. Still others spend freely, certain their ship will dock soon and be laden with inheritance, sudden recognition and financial reward, or the prize-patrol bunch. They don't plan, and they certainly don't plan on something coming along that might sink their ship. They deny the urgency of money management or wise spending choices, and bet on tomorrow; things will always be better by tomorrow. Or by next month. Or by this time next year. Let me bring this fallacy home with the true story of Aunt Peg.

My husband's Aunt Peg was a well-to-do spinster who was legendary for her crusty demeanor—and big heart. Many,

many people found their way to Peg's door, and never left empty-handed. Everyone knew that Peg had money. Although Peg assured my husband he would be "taken care of" when she died, we never once considered any of her wealth in our future plans, mostly because we were more interested in Aunt Peg living. No daydreams were built around financial liberty at some date, as Peg grew older and older and began to lose cognition. Unable to care for herself, and not recognizing those most precious to her, Peg lived her remaining life in a nursing home. The cost of care relieved her of all her money until, years later, she died in a state of near-poverty. We were able to mourn the loss of Aunt Peg, and not fret over dashed dreams.

Don't Wait Another Minute!

It takes gumption and strength of character to look your situation in the eye and face the music. If you are in financial trouble, you must take action *now*. The journey of a thousand miles, said a Chinese philosopher, begins with the first step.

Open your mail.

This one giant step will make all the next steps on your path to financial security much easier. For now, this little exercise in terror serves one purpose alone: to force you to put long-term and short-term debt on paper and have a good long look at it. Once you assess your money situation, you can find ways to improve it or to seek the help you need. We will look closely at monthly bills and living expenses in future chapters. Some of you, because of discipline and wise planning, will be able to fill in the provided chart with ease. (You may use the chart in this book or copy it on a separate sheet of paper.)

Before reading further, fill in the following chart and answer the questions below:

Type of Debt	Total Amount of Debt	Monthly Payment	Interest Rate	Number of Months Remaining
MORTGAGE				
AUTOMOBILE				
SHORT-TERM LOAN				
CREDIT CARD				
ITEMIZE OTHER DEBT				
TOTAL				

Bravo for you—just for getting through this chart! Take heart if you are frightened by the amount of debt you have amassed. Once you apply sound money management principles from this book (or others like it) you will move farther and farther away from debt and closer and closer to financial security. Stick to it! The hardest part is over. (And while this may seem a little brutal of me right now, let's try to really bring home any predicament you might be in—just for some added incentive!)

Tea *Time!*

I am considering making a consolidation loan (or already have) to pay off my debt. ☐ yes ☐ no

I am consistently late with payments. ☐ yes ☐ no

I obtain new credit cards so I can transfer my balance from an existing credit card. ☐ yes ☐ no

I cannot pay more than the minimum payment required each month. ☐ yes ☐ no

I have no budget, or I consistently fall off the one I have. ☐ yes ☐ no

I have no savings (or the balance in my savings is shrinking). ☐ yes ☐ no

I do not live within my means. ☐ yes ☐ no

Debt reduction (not counting mortgage/rent) is more than 20 percent of my/our net income. ☐ yes ☐ no

I want to tithe, but there is absolutely no money to do so. ☐ yes ☐ no

I am frightened by my mail and by the ringing of a phone.
☐ yes ☐ no
I am in complete despair over financial circumstances.
☐ yes ☐ no

If you answered yes to any of the above questions, you are probably in a little trouble—and you are not alone! Many others like you have found themselves in financial hot water. The good news is that if you roll up your sleeves and apply some simple principles to your situation, you are on your way out of that pit of despair.

What Kind of Trouble Are You In?

Down-and-Out

Either through unemployment, disability, divorce, or the death of your spouse, some of you are in grave financial trouble. I know how you feel, and I can tell you with the absolute certainty of someone who has been in your shoes: *You will pull through this.* Grip your bootstraps with your teeth if you have to, and keep pressing on.

I cannot stress strongly enough that *God cares.* Turn to him. Some of you may feel that if he cared, you wouldn't be in this situation in the first place. That is an honest response. When I look back, I can see sinful and destructive behavior on my part, and on the part of others, that combined to create my situation. It certainly wasn't clear back then! I can also see (two decades later) a heavenly Father who loved me so much that he stripped me of everything I had—to get my attention. I am now grateful for the hardship I endured. It is crystal clear to me now that he was with me all along, and it was during this time of suffering that I began to turn to him in earnest.

Scripture tells us in Matthew 6:33 to seek first the kingdom of God, and he will take care of the rest. We must learn to set our eyes on heaven. Jesus points to the Father, and speaks of the Father's tender care, when he says: "Which of you, if his son asks for bread, will give him a stone?" (Matthew 7:9).

You may be thinking you'd settle for a stone—for anything—just to know you are not forsaken by God. Let me ask you this: Suppose you were in school and the teacher handed you a test? Sometimes, dear child of God, your teacher trusts you enough to leave the room while you take that test.

Seek help. Start by asking your church for help and support. Be willing to make yourself financially accountable to someone. Look in the phone book for community-based nonprofit or state-based agencies. Such groups as United Way, Salvation Army, or Catholic Charities often have a call-in line for people in need. They will provide you a safety net, and most likely network you with other important agencies or programs until you can get on your feet. If you are in a community with no such agencies, call the local police department. There is help for you.

Special Note: If you are down-and-out, and either pregnant or postpartum, and have children, it is absolutely critical that you do what is necessary to get proper nutrition for yourself and your child. WIC (Women, Infants, and Children) is a federal government program designed to help you.

Extra Special Note: If you are suffering from domestic violence, please seek help. You do not deserve to be abused. Go to your pastor, or call the Domestic Violence Hotline: Call directory assistance at 1-800-555-1212 to obtain their current 800 number.

More Outgo Than Income

If you are not beset by down-and-out problems, then there are two reasons for your dilemma: You mismanage the money you have, or your lifestyle is too costly for your income. If you mismanage money, this book will help you to understand principles of budgeting, shopping, and saving. If your lifestyle is too costly, you may have to make changes.

Remember Jan from the first chapter? One of my recommendations to her was that she sell her high-priced house and purchase something just as suitable, but less expensive. I pointed out that the car she was leaning against probably set her back a bit each month, too. If Jan reduced the choke-hold her house and car payments had on her, she would have considerably more liquidity.

My husband and I used to live in a modest little home, but we had to pay exorbitant property tax because of our location. As much as we liked our cabin on the lake, we recently faced hard facts: It was too taxing to our budget (and perhaps an unwise use of money) to stay where we were. We sold our cabin and moved to a home that allowed us to live within our means.

Are you willing to do the same?

Shopped Till You Dropped, So You Crawl

There are a couple of reasons for this problem. One is cultural. We have been trained by Madison Avenue hype to shop as recreation and for relaxation. Every year we have new models, improved formulas, and this season's colors. Nonstop advertising convinces us never to be satisfied, always to want; it tells us we will find inner peace with that one more thing. If you shop till you drop, then stop! If you want recreation, go to the park. If you want to relax, brew some tea, grab a library book, and put up your feet. Read about the difference between need and want.

The other reason for nonstop shopping is addiction. Because of unsettled, unidentified, and even unrecognized emotional problems, many of us spend money on ourselves or on others to ease our pain, to find acceptance, to resolve inner turmoil. In her book *When Spending Takes the Place of Feeling*, Karen O'Connor writes:

Most shopping addicts are living out someone else's "should system"—their mothers', a celebrity's, a manufacturer's, a designer's, a friend's. They are dealing with psychological and social influences so great they cannot even consider them, much less face and deal with them. Issues of low self-esteem, lack of boundaries, and problems with reality are all part of the complex behavior that plays itself out in a shopping frenzy.[2]

If you believe you have an addiction to shopping or spending unwisely, seek God's grace to liberate you from this bondage. Counselors, also, can help you sort through your behavior and lead you biblically toward freedom. Check with your church, or consult with other churches until you find a Christian professional. Consider, too, the confidence of a close friend. If you have a friend who is strong and supportive, ask if you might be accountable to that person during this time of healing.

Indebted-Mess

Good people end up in debt. And I don't just mean mortgage and car payments. For as many reasons as there are snowflakes, some of us have fallen in a dizzying spiral until we have joined rank and file at pit bottom. But we haven't figured out how to find our footing. We need help, and we need it now.

All of the enthusiasm and determination in the world isn't going to stop the bill collector from closing in. Your confidence is maxed just like your credit line. You are horrified at the prospect of bankruptcy, but feel that is the only solution. If you are on the edge of bankruptcy and cannot work your way out on your own, there is help. Consumer Credit Counseling Services (CCCS) is a not-for-profit organization with over seven hundred offices nationwide. Look in your Yellow Pages for the number of an office near you. If you are overwhelmed with debt, or if you just need someone to guide you through the maze of budgeting, money management, and planned debt liquidation, these people might be able to help.

Suddenly On Your Own

You may suddenly have found yourself widowed or divorced; not down-and-out, but perhaps terrified at the financial consequence of your new situation, or bewildered about taking your first tentative steps. This book has an entire chapter written just for you. (See chapter nine.)

Doing Quite Nicely, Thank You

Suppose you are getting along quite well financially, and just need to earn a merit badge in advanced financial planning? You may pay your bills promptly, and might even have some money tucked away in an old sock. There may be, however, specific goals and objectives you intend to get around to. You *intend* to meet with a lawyer, and protect your heirs. You *intend* to diversify your savings portfolio. The time is now, but how do you carry out your intentions?

How Now! Figure Out Where You Are Going

I am notorious in my family for my lousy sense of direction. It's not uncommon for me to lose myself in a mall. I need a road map to find my way out of a parking lot! Send me to the moon and I'll end up on Mars. If your financial management has been without direction—if you do not know where you are going—and your route to financial security is more like the flight to Mars, you need *a plan!*

Tea *Time!*

Here is your first project: Invest in a new spiral notebook, sit down undisturbed (couples should squirrel away together someplace), and get ready to put everything on paper. You are going to write a business plan. From now on, think of yourself as partner or sole-proprietor of "The Smith Family, Inc." or "Mrs. Smith, Ltd." or "The Ms. Smith Co."

Every successful business has a plan that usually consists of four parts:

1. The mission statement, or *objective*
2. The overall *plan* that pursues the objective
3. The *action* it takes to make the plan viable to pursue the objective
4. The *review*

Let's be silly for a while and go back to when I was nine, and picked wildflowers to sell. Suppose I had a business plan. What might it look like?

Objective: To make some spending money so Mom can take us for a Sunday ride and I can order a double-dip ice cream cone! *Plan:* Sell flowers door-to-door to neighbors: Find patches of wildflowers, decorate old baby buggy, pick out neighbors who have bought from me in the past, do this all before Saturday morning.

Action: Pick flowers on Saturday morning, bundle them with string, stack bundles in baby buggy, peddle to neighbors on Saturday afternoon, get home in time for *The Adventures of Superman. Special note*: Be sure to bring Biffy to protect me from neighborhood dogs, especially that mean Shep up the street.

Review: Count my loot. Give to Mom. Think about how I can keep the flowers from drooping and hanging off my hand like cooked spaghetti. Give Biffy a bone.

Now It's Your Turn

Establishing Your Financial Objective

Start with your objective. Team up with your husband, if that is possible. Take a few days to think about this. Pour a cup or two of tea. Read Proverbs 31. Your objective should be short, concise, and from the heart.

Here are some examples:

- I want to be out of debt in _____ years.
- My family will learn to be content with a simpler, less consumptive lifestyle.
- The mortgage will be paid in full by _____.
- I/We will get the kids through college without student loans.
- I will go barging in France next summer.
- I/We will become better stewards of possessions *and* spiritual gifts.

What is your objective? _____

_____

_____

Making Your Plan

Now you need a plan. There is an old saying that goes something like this: Many people plan to fail because they fail to plan. You must plan to succeed. Many financial experts claim that even though some Americans manage to save money, *even those who do save* lack any formal strategy for doing so—increasing the chance that they will fall short of their financial goals. The bottom line: Planning results in better savings.

1. Your plan should be specific, measurable, and have a time line. If, for instance, you want to get out of debt in five years, you might say:

> To be out of debt in five years I will have to learn to live within my means. To do that, I will have to develop a realistic monthly budget, get out from under the burden of car payments, change my attitude, and sacrificially apply excess income to debt reduction.

2. While developing your plan, be sure you answer two questions: *why* you are in debt, and *how* you are going to get out of debt. Figure out why you are in the situation you're in. Here are some examples.

Why I am in debt:
- The lure of easy credit is so tempting that I make purchases when I shouldn't.
- At times, I could have certainly gotten along with less, but didn't.
- At times, I could have given a homemade gift or card.
- At times, I could have gone *without* rather than use my charge card.
- I just *had* to get that new car—after all, the old one needed a lot of repair.

What can you add to the list? _____
_____
_____

How I am going to get out of debt:
- I will cut up all but one credit card.

- I will discipline myself to use my one card wisely or not at all.
- I will develop a payment plan and stick to it as best I can.
- I will learn to be content with little, or less, and become creative with what I have.
- I will do all of this through the guidance and help of God the Holy Spirit.
- I will not become a tightfisted grump, but a smart steward. I will do this by learning everything I can about money management and consumer spending.

What is your plan? _____

_____

_____

Taking Action

Now you need an action statement. Daily, weekly, or monthly lists, or action plans, will help you keep a good perspective. Here are some ideas:

- I will write a letter today rather than talk long-distance, or today I will begin to limit my long-distance calls.
- This week I will say no, half the time, to impulse buying, eating out, and unnecessary shopping.
- This month, I will see what I can save by eliminating or increasing insurance deductibles.
- I will explore the possibility of rewriting the mortgage.
- I will become a "utilities detective" and determine where (and how) I can save money on electricity, gas (including gasoline for the car!), oil, phone, garbage, and water bills.

Write your action statement: _____

_____

_____

Review Your Plan

4. The final aspect to your business plan is periodic review and modification. Develop a system of looking at your plan and determining your progress. Do this at least monthly (weekly until you are in the groove). Once you begin to monitor and track your spending (see chapter three), you will have material to review. (My husband and I meet weekly when we feel ourselves slipping toward sloppy spending behavior.)

A Plan for the Grand Scheme of Things

Suppose you wrote an objective for life. What kinds of plans and actions would you need to consider if your objective were to sail through life debt-free and financially secure?

There are general objectives that apply to just about anyone, and most of these guidelines are age-specific. You will be headed in the right direction if you use this list as an easy measurement.

Twenty-something

- Establish a credit rating by paying bills on time, taking out a loan in your name, developing a good rapport with a bank.
- Make saving money a matter-of-fact principle in your life

by starting a savings account. When you have enough saved, open a small money-market fund or a CD (Certificate of Deposit). Keep expanding and investing what you earn through savings.

- Develop an ironclad determination to always maintain a certain amount in an emergency fund. Do this with saved money that can be accessed easily.

- Buy life insurance when you are young (the younger you are, the less expensive the premiums).

- Make sure you have a will. Find a lawyer who will take you seriously. It is an important matter to develop the discipline to make a will, or if you have a will, to review it. If you have children, you will want to be the one to choose their guardian.

- Begin to save/plan for your first home. The down payment will come from disciplined savings and smart investments.

- If you have children, look into your options for long-term growth investments, so college will be funded when that time rolls around. (And it will before you know it!)

Thirty-something

- Be sure your assets are protected from any loss, be it catastrophic, such as fire, or from rising income tax, or poorly planned estate settlement in the event of death. Do this through proper insurance coverage on possessions (adjusted to keep up with inflation), taking advantage of tax-deferred investments, and meeting with a professional to evaluate the necessity for estate protection.

- Don't stop saving now! "Retirement" will enter your

mind more often. Get maximum benefit from retirement plans provided by employment, or from a plan geared to those who work at home (including mommies!).

- Make sure your will is up-to-date, especially if you have children, or if there have been changes in your life, such as divorce, or a move to another state.

Forty-something

- Your personal income may be "taxing." You may have to consult with an accountant or financial planning expert to shield your paycheck from escalating taxes.
- Don't stop saving now! "Retirement" is a word you use more and more! Hurry up and start saving if you haven't started yet.
- Make sure the insurance on assets such as your home is current. Make a video tape of the contents of your home, or write an inventory of possessions.
- Check the will again! And talk with a lawyer about whether or not a trust is a good idea, to protect the kids in case you die.

Fifty-something

- Don't stop saving now! "Retirement" is right around the corner! You are in the home stretch, so begin to make your final plans for that golden moment. Figure out how much money you will need; think about whether you want to stay put or relocate, when you are free to go.
- Meet with a financial expert, and discuss whether you should consolidate your investments if they are hard to liquidate.

- Make sure your will and estate plan are current! Check and double-check your life and health insurance policies, and begin to plan supplementation if it will be necessary.

Sixty-something and beyond
- Definitely don't stop saving now! Be prepared for whatever comes your way. This is when proper planning and organization (starting when you were twenty-something) pays off. Keep some growth investments, otherwise consider keeping yourself liquid and with safer, fixed-income investments.
- Revise your will and keep your estate plan at the ready! Leave your heirs a legacy, not a lump of coal. Consult with a trusted *and experienced* attorney.
- Be absolutely certain your health and life insurance is adequate to protect your assets from costly medical expenses. Consult a trusted *and experienced* agent.

Now I Lay Me Down to Sleep, to Lay These Problems at Your Feet

Before bed tonight, there is one more important exercise for you to do. Find a quiet spot, pick a time when you won't be interrupted, and write a prayer to God the Father. Share your deepest worry, problem, or sinful behavior. Write it all out. He knows already, so it is fruitless to keep anything from him. He wants your trust, he wants your attention, he wants your heart.

When you pray, keep in mind that you may have to suffer some consequence. There may have to be a few words of repentance in that prayer of yours, along with a heartfelt and sincere pledge to overcome greed, or covetousness, or lack of control. Will God give you the grace to overcome? He promised he would. Will he bail you out of the mess you are in? Maybe. Or maybe he will let you suffer the consequences of your actions.

I remember when our son, Josh, stole a pack of gum. He was six years old and knew he was pilfering. When I discovered the misdeed, I strongly reprimanded him. Wasn't that punishment enough? No. I had to allow (and force) my beloved child to suffer through the agony of admitting his theft to the store manager, apologizing, and then paying for the gum with money I insisted he earn. Was my heart filled with the same agony as Josh's? Yes, it was.

Money and Thee: Finding Your Way

The two most important principles for you to memorize right now are: God is not a grump, and he knows your heart. If you turn to him in earnest, by turning *over* everything to him, he will supply the grace and mercy you need to brave your financial battle. The first skirmish—facing reality—is over. You've even mapped out your next "plan of attack." Now you need to build up your arsenal with a strong left hook to the pocketbook: You need a budget.

Now it's your turn to write. Think about what you have read in this chapter. How does it apply to you? Soul-search a little, and jot down your thoughts.

Where I am now: _____

_____

_____

Where I'd like to be: _____

_____

_____

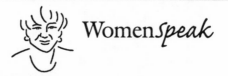 Women*Speak*

"Figuring out a budget and sticking with it (my mother prefers to call it 'planned spending') is how I live within my means. I keep what I'm going to spend in my checking account, and put the rest in savings (which has a big 'Don't touch' sign on it) as soon as I get my paycheck."

———

"The biggest mistake I've ever made when it comes to money is not keeping track of receipts, so that I know how I am spending my money. This includes incidentals, which tend to add up."

———

"My secret for living within my means is knowing what my 'means' are. Most people don't really know."

———

"My secret to living within my means is a family budget. With so many of today's recurring bills being paid electronically, we can budget ourselves closely and never be late. What is left over after fixed expenses is ours to lavish on groceries and gasoline. Another *big* help is a pretax flexible spending account for nonreimbursed medical and dental expenses. It's way too easy to skip those checkups and new glasses if you don't have the bucks tucked away."

———

"My husband and I set up a budget together. Whenever he wants to spend more than we've planned (which is about six days of the week!), I remind him that *he* agreed on the budget, too. If he keeps nagging me, I ask him if we need to refigure our budget. That prospect pretty much solves the problem!"

three

To Budge or Not to Budge, There Is No Question

A budget is like meatloaf. Meatloaf requires certain ingredients; what you add to the basics depends on your recipe. And every cook has her own concoction.

Budgets are like that. You have certain fixed expenses that must be paid. And then there are extra expenses, making your budget unique to you. Your budget is your recipe, and it can be as homemade or as store-bought as you like.

In your budget, you set limits and prioritize. A budget is how much you plan in advance to spend.

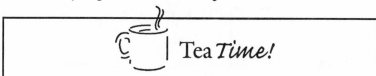 Tea *Time!*

What has been your experience with a budget?
a. Did great until I heard my mother-in-law was coming for a two-week stay, then blew a bundle decorating.
b. Did great until the President's Day Sale at Shoptilyoudrop & Co.
c. Never tried, because I face each paycheck with a shrug and "What bills do I have to pay this month?" thoughts.
d. All of the above.

In the last chapter you faced your situation square in the pocketbook. Whether you needed smelling salts, or congratu-

lated yourself for a job well done, your work has just begun:
Either you need to get out of the mess you are in, or you need
to keep your ship afloat. It's time to make a budget.

First, we must take the threat out of the idea of budgeting.
To do that, I will start with a confession: Joe and I have a "sort-
of" budget. I am telling you now so you won't be intimidated
by this chapter, and because we think "sort-of" budgets are just
fine for the right personality. I call ours "sort-of" because we
don't like the rigidity of don't-*budge*-from-it money management that reduces some people to tightwads and skinflints.
(How many of us have run into characters who are miserly with
every penny they pinch?) *Lots* of people succeed with a "sort-
of" budget.

Tea *Time!*

Can excessive attention to budgeting be a form of love of
money?
Hint: Where is your focus?

The word *budget* has gained a reputation it does not
deserve. Why? Because so many of us woke one fine morning,
enthusiastically declared we were on a budget, and blew it by
noon. The analogy has been made zillions of times, but *budget*
and *diet* probably take the award as the two most dreaded
words-in-common with everyone else on the planet. They certainly rank as the two top items we resolve to get control of
when we make New Year's resolutions (right up there with
flossing our teeth), except in most households these goals are

never met. Why? Because we don't know what we're doing, and we refuse to budge.

Have you ever gone on a diet? Hah! you say, your life *is* a diet! So let me ask you this: If you've been on a diet all your life, how come you're not thin like a thermometer? Can it be that you're going about your diet in a way that doesn't bring success? Same principle. Have you handled money all your life? Then, how come you aren't living within your means? Can it be that many of us haven't learned what skills we need to be successful?

Know when I am successful at losing weight? When I write down every morsel that enters my fat, puckered lips. Or when I cut back on food consumption. With money, same principle, squared. When you write down where every dollar goes, then you know how much money you need in order to get along, and when to cut back on spending.

"Tracking" money is an age-old method used to evaluate spending habits and to reveal good (and bad) spending patterns. *It is a time for scrupulous honesty.* It's easy to track fixed expenses, so we'll start there.

Getting on Track

Grab that spiral notebook you bought for chapter two, or use the chart below. *Write down your in-cement monthly expenses.* (Your checkbook register will help immensely.) For instance, just about every one of us pays mortgage or rent, and we certainly pay utilities, phone, or maintenance. Many of us have loan payments or tuition. Most of us have less-frequent bills, such as taxes and insurance, so factor in a realistic monthly allotment for those payments.

In-Cement Expense	Monthly Payment	Estimated Monthly Allotment
TITHE		
SAVINGS		
MORTGAGE/RENT		
CAR PAYMENT(S)		
ELECTRICITY (BUDGET PLAN)		
HEAT		
TELEPHONE (BASIC SERVICE)		
INTERNET PROVIDER FEE		
WATER		
GARBAGE SERVICE		
AUTO INSURANCE		
HOMEOWNERS' INSURANCE		
HEALTH INSURANCE		
LIFE INSURANCE		
CHILDCARE		
TUITION		
PROPERTY TAXES		
CAR LICENSES/FEES		
LOAN PAYMENTS		
DEBT REDUCTION PAYMENTS		
ALIMONY/CHILD SUPPORT		
OTHER		
OTHER		
TOTAL		

Now here comes a tall order: *Track all your unfixed, or variable, expenses.* I recommend keeping a journal of all expenditures for at least one month (two months is best). Once you've tracked all expenditures, you will be able to sit down and calculate where your money goes. (*Now* it's time for the smelling salts! Unless someone is unwisely living in a home that's too costly, or driving a car they can't afford, I'm convinced it's in this rather unregulated area of money management where we end up in trouble.)

A normal day might look like this:

- gasoline: $12
- toll booth: $1
- brought lunch, bought pop: $.75
- rented videos: $2.50
- gave kids money for Little League: $10

If your husband refuses to participate in this venture, engage in some guesswork and try to track expenses on your own. This is an excellent opportunity for some relational building and communications skills. You might lead into the subject with one of the following lines:

- What if we could come up with more cash each month with no extra work on your part?
- I'll bet you a jar of dill pickles that you can't remember where you spent money today!
- It would mean a lot to me if we could read Luke 16:10-13 together and talk about its application to our lives. (Have a good commentary on hand.)

Once you track expenditures (don't try to be good yet), you will have an idea of how much you pay for other necessities (and not-so-necessary necessities.) Tracking expenses helps you evaluate monthly expenditure for the following: food; clothes;

laundry/dry cleaning; gasoline; car maintenance/tolls/parking; eating out; walking-around-money for wife and husband; medicine; doctor/dentist; gifts; home maintenance; personal improvement; pets; baby sitter; newspapers/magazines; recreation; travel; children's expenses, including school lunches, allowance, clubs/activities; other.

You must know what you are spending, and you must be honest about it!

Tea *Time!*

Challenge yourself to go one entire day without spending money unnecessarily.

Then bump it up to two days; then three.

Uh-Oh!

I know; I know—I told you the hard part was over once you faced your circumstance squarely. But I never said there wouldn't be hard work ahead for you! Tracking your expenditures and writing them down is a *very good* thing.

Joe and I have tracked our spending on and off for years, and we have developed a second-nature when it comes to latitudes in spending. For instance, I have a monthly budget of $100 for food. (Sounds insane, but we get along quite nicely.)

Do I follow the monthly budget to the penny? Of course not! I am simply so practiced at food purchase, storage, and preparation that I can go weeks without grocery shopping, and I always have a "sense" if I am getting out of bounds. Do I sometimes go over budget? Of course. But it is more than compensated for during the months that I go into my "use things up" frenzy. (I am writing this chapter in late spring. Spring means one thing around here: Use what's in the freezer to make room for the new harvest a few months away.)

Another example: Joe and I rarely eat dinner in a restaurant, but we like to go out for breakfast. Does Joe hit the panic button and pull out his pocket calculator if I order one bagel too many? No. We eat out within reason. We've done this for so many years that we instinctively know when to skip the extra bagel. I'd wager that you already do the same thing in many little ways.

Prioritize

I don't believe budgeting is as easy as pie—I'm talking about the pie charts that tell you what percentage to spend on what. They are good guides, but we set ourselves up for failure if we do not tailor-make our spending and savings plan. Go back to the charts and study your spending habits. Where do you overspend? Where can you cut back? Where can you sacrifice? What is important to you? We're all different. For example:

- Myrtle would rather eat oatmeal for dinner five nights a week than lose her membership in the local clog-dancing club.
- Samantha is eyeing retirement, only a few years away.
- Darlene is willing to sacrifice so Junior can take oboe lessons.
- Kathryn's husband is in graduate school. She works hard to keep them afloat. Their apartment in the country does not have laundry facilities. Laundromat duty is draining for both of them. It's worth the sacrifice in other areas to have their clothes washed by the laundry. At seventy-five

cents a pound, however, they are diligent not to soil many clothes.

Look at your expense-tracking record. Put a smile next to the expenditures that are important to you or your family. Now look at all the entries. Would the world stop spinning if you didn't have an espresso every morning? Would your husband join the French Foreign Legion (and take the kids) if you got creative with leftovers? Would a romp in the leaves, and a walk around the neighborhood (or other creative cost-free recreation) do, instead of a costly trip to the movies? Put a frown next to expenses that can be reduced or eliminated.

Joe takes delight in buying me a mint patty on his way home from work. Suppose he did that every night. The candy costs fifty cents (and brings a whopping 170 calories)! That equals $10 a month, or $120 a year! Not to mention 40,800 calories! Yikes! I better have a talk with that man!

The In-Box

Now that you know how much you spend, you need to look at how much you earn. Summarize all income, from every source:

salary #1 _____	salary #2 _____		
child support _____	alimony _____		
interest _____	dividends _____		
other _____	other _____		
Subtotal _____	+ Subtotal _____	=	_____

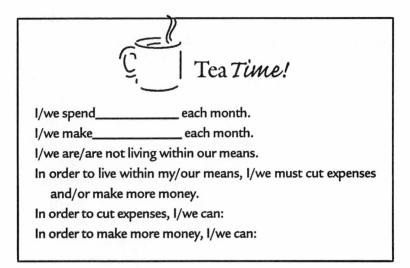

Tea *Time!*

I/we spend_____ each month.
I/we make_____ each month.
I/we are/are not living within our means.
In order to live within my/our means, I/we must cut expenses
    and/or make more money.
In order to cut expenses, I/we can:
In order to make more money, I/we can:

Behavior Plus Balance Equals Blessing

If you are saying, "B...b...but..." right now, think back to the meatloaf. Meatloaf is bland without salt. If a little salt is good, a whole lot is better, right? No. Because too much salt spoils the recipe. You've learned balance in cooking; learn it in money management. Too much freedom or too much rigidity spoils the budget process, and you lose heart.

Approach your budget plans with balance in perspectives, goals, and achievements. Allow for a little living; allow for a little backsliding. Always be prepared to pick yourself up, dust yourself off, and start over. Plan in advance how much you will spend on whim, fancy, or necessity. Work to change b...b...but into b...b...blessing!

Behavior plus balance equals blessing. If you are obedient to the clear commands from Scripture to faithfully manage your money (and possessions and gifts and time), you will find peace and prosperity, even in the poorest circumstance.

Does that mean you are not in God's will if things aren't going well for you? Not necessarily. (But if you are not being a good and sensible steward of what he has given you materially and in the area of your talents, that may be exactly what it means!) Does that mean that if you tithe, you will never have problems or have to worry about finances? No. God never promises that our life will be trouble-free. Your impoverished condition may become a blessing to you and others, later in life, or your situation may be the result of someone else's sinful behavior. Remember my period of desperation, when I was broke, and responsible for my son? That was twenty years ago. I view that now as the greatest blessing of my life, for it was then that I first put my trust in God, and gave my life to Jesus.

It is important for us to be disciplined in all areas of financial management. How we own, buy, spend, and save demonstrates our understanding of Scripture and our obedience to its precepts.

What's So Biblical About Handling Money?

Ron Blue claims the Bible contains over two thousand references to money.[1] I've never counted them, but I believe they are there. Proverbs 21:5 is a perfect teaching for a chapter on budgeting: "The plans of the diligent lead to profit as surely as haste leads to poverty." Eugene Peterson paraphrased this verse: "Careful planning puts you ahead in the long run; hurry and scurry puts you further behind" (*The Message*).

Christians find comfort, promise, and peace in the Bible.

Scripture, however, is more than the salvation message—it is also instruction. Yes, God so loved the world that he gave his only begotten Son. He also so loved the world that he gave us unmistakable guidelines to enable us to cope and manage in a broken and fallen world. It is a grievous error for people to regard the Bible as a finger-wagging, scowling, heartless set of rules. God is love, and he loves his children.

Jesus (God incarnate) taught: "Which of you, if his son asks for bread, will give him a stone? Or if he asks for a fish, will give him a snake? If you, then, though you are evil, know how to give good gifts to your children, how much more will your Father in heaven give good gifts to those who ask him!" (Matthew 7: 9-11).

God created us, and set forth instruction that will bring us peace and joy and closer communion with him. When we are in accord with his will and follow his guidance, we will succeed.

Two clear directives in the Bible represent two expenses that are sometimes overlooked when making a budget: tithing and savings. (Savings gets a whole chapter of its own.)

Tithing—Or—The Lord Letting Me Keep 90 Percent
We are told to give a tenth of what we earn back to God:

> Be sure to set aside a tenth of all that your fields produce each year.... At the end of every three years, bring all the tithes of that year's produce and store it in your towns, so that the Levites (who have no allotment or inheritance of their own) and the aliens, the fatherless and the widows who live in your towns may come and eat and be satisfied, and so that the Lord your God may bless you in all the work of your hands.
>
> DEUTERONOMY 14:22, 28-29

God is not a harsh taskmaster. He literally invites us to try to outgive him! There is one place in the Bible where we are told it's OK to test, or challenge, God (see Malachi 3:10).

Malachi was a prophet to Israel after its exile, and during a time of shattered hopes. As Israel returned from exile, religious fervor waned, and things just didn't seem to be going as they had expected. Malachi used their failure to tithe as a demonstration of their failure to worship God completely:

> "I the Lord do not change. So you, O descendants of Jacob, are not destroyed. Ever since the time of your forefathers you have turned away from my decrees and have not kept them. Return to me, and I will return to you," says the Lord Almighty.
>
> "But you ask, 'How are we to return?'
>
> "Will a man rob God? Yet you rob me.
>
> "But you ask, 'How do we rob you?'
>
> "In tithes and offerings....Bring the whole tithe into the storehouse....Test me in this;" says the Lord Almighty; "and see if I will not throw open the floodgates of heaven and pour out so much blessing that you will not have room enough for it."
>
> MALACHI 3:6-10

In dealing with the Jews, God pointed out that he will remain faithful to those who seek him with all their heart...and with their pocketbook. The tithe was law to the Jew. Violation of that law was not just an expression of selfishness, but of a breakdown of the covenant relationship they had with God. It was disobedience. Yet God says: Hah! You think you can outgive me? Return to me, I haven't moved. I am here. Make a go of it, restore your dependence upon me, exhibit your trust in me, and the blessings will come.

Are we to tithe so we get blessings in return? Not if our hearts are right. We are to tithe because we're told to tithe. If our motives are pure and just, God will honor his promise to open the floodgates of heaven, because the Lord our God does not change. And he does not lie.

Some of you may be thinking, *That's the Law; I'm under grace!* Yes, you are. And the debt of grace is so much greater than the debt of Law. The Law compels; grace impels. You were bought with a price immeasurable—you owe him *everything.*

On one of his teaching tapes, the late Dr. Walter Martin discusses the fact that the principle of tithing appears in the New Testament.[2] Hebrews 7 tells the story of how Abraham, the father of the Jews, gave honor and tithe to Melchizedek, long before the law to tithe was given through Moses. Jesus, according to the book of Hebrews, is the great, indestructible high priest, in the order of Melchizedek.

Hebrews 7 goes on to say that Levi was "still in the body of his ancestor (Abraham)." In other words, as the father of the Jews, Abraham represented all heirs of the covenant. Galatians, a New Testament letter written to Gentiles, says, "If you belong to Christ, then you are Abraham's seed, and heirs according to the promise" (3:29). Shall we claim the promises of Abraham, but not pay the tithe of Abraham?

Jesus taught us that it is more blessed to give than to receive, because in giving, we receive. What, therefore, is our responsibility to God?

Charitable giving should be at the center of a Christian's heart. Joe and I believe in tithing to our church. We support a local ministry, also, and look at extra income as an opportunity for God to bless someone in need. We recently sold an old pump for $150. It was nice to have the extra money, but it was exciting to wonder to whom the Lord intended for us to give $15!

Try to Save 10 Percent, and Live on 80 Percent!
You're probably thinking, *Hey! I bought this book because I don't have enough money to go around, and you want me to tithe AND save money?* Yep. You will be glad I insisted on this. We will talk much more about savings later, but I needed to mention it in the budget chapter. There is always, I repeat ALWAYS, going to be a good reason not to put aside money in savings.

Family Circle called Oseola McCarty "America's Most Generous Woman." This woman donated her life savings to start a college scholarship fund. Oseola worked hard all of her life, washing other people's clothes, to make a living. This is what she says about saving money: "I started saving when I was a little girl, just to have candy money. When I got grown, I started saving for my future. I'd go to the bank once a month, and hold out just enough to cover my expenses, then put the rest into my savings account....It's not the ones that make the big money, but the ones who know how to save who get ahead."[3]

Heed this advice, especially if you are young. Teach it to your children. *We must learn to tithe, to save, and to live within our means.*

Ready, Set, Budge!

Time for the rubber to meet the road. We've talked about the need to budget. You've tracked and evaluated your monthly spending patterns. You've considered behavior and balance, and are certainly ready for blessings! You recognize the command to tithe, and the importance of saving.

Sharpen your pencil, roll up your sleeves, arm yourself with your financial data, pray for guidance, and design your budget. To do this, you could:

1. Buy a budget workbook. Fill in the blanks.
2. Go to the library and borrow a workbook. Transfer the information to a tablet at home.
3. Buy a user-friendly computer program.
4. Use the popular envelope system. Put allocated funds in envelopes labeled with different categories—food; entertainment; clothing; personal care, including haircuts.
5. Set some rules:
   - Don't borrow from food to fatten entertainment.
   - At the end of the month, put leftover funds in savings, or toward debt reduction.
   - When the envelope is empty, it stays empty till the next budget cycle.

When Earnestine Earnestly Decided to Budget

For the sake of illustration, let's create a woman on a budget mission. We'll call her Earnestine. She is a single mom with two kids. She works, and brings home $1,000 every two weeks.

As you can see, Earnestine has tithing down pat. This principle was taught to her by godly parents. Earnestine has been tithing all her life.

Earnestine is *really* trying to save. To make the effort a little easier, she has authorized that every pay period, $50 be automatically deposited into a mutual fund account. She strives toward the goal of saving 10 percent of her net income, but just cannot handle that right now. She has found a budget to be more *help* than burden, and uses it to identify problem spending. If she can master the problems, she is certain she'll be able to add more to her monthly savings. (As you can see, Earnestine has a tendency to get a bit long-winded on the telephone.)

Because she was tracking her food expenses for the month, Earnestine realized that she was over budget at the end of the third week. She began creating meals out of the groceries she had in the cupboard, rather than pick up packaged food at the grocery store. All she had to buy was fruit, eggs, and milk.

Earnestine has been trying to drive her car in a more resourceful manner, avoiding backtracking when she runs errands, or unnecessary trips. For the few months she's been on her budget, she has consistently gone over on gasoline, making her think she was a bit unrealistic when allocating funds. She's thinking of changing her gasoline allotment to $55 each month. She may do just that. In the meantime, she's going to write letters to her long-distance friends.

EXPENSE	WEEK 1	WEEK 2	WEEK 3	WEEK 4	TOTAL	ALLOCATED	COMMENTS
Tithe	50	50	50	50	200	200	Yay!
Savings/Retirement	0	50	0	50	100	200	Uh-Oh!
Telephone				103	103	50	Yikes!
Food	79	43	81	11	214	200	Uh-Oh!
Gasoline/Oil	14	12	17	14	57	50	Uh-Oh!

How Earnest Are You?

If you earnestly want to embark on your own budget mission, the following chart may help you. It lists several spending categories, representing weekly, monthly, quarterly, or yearly financial obligations. You may use this information to create a system unique to your circumstances. Please consider keeping the "Uh-oh!" and the "Yay!" in whatever system you choose—a little incentive or a little affirmation might help you stretch your dollars just a wee bit more!

EXPENSE	WEEK 1	WEEK 2	WEEK 3	WEEK 4	TOTAL	ALLOCATED	COMMENTS
Tithe							
Savings/Retirement							
Mortgage/Rent							
Property Tax							
Home Repair/Upkeep							
Home Insurance							
Food at Home							
Food Away							
Electric/Gas/Other							
Water/Sewer/Garbage							
Cable TV							
Telephone							
Car Payment							
Car Repair/Upkeep							
Gasoline/Oil							

EXPENSE	WEEK 1	WEEK 2	WEEK 3	WEEK 4	TOTAL	ALLOCATED	COMMENTS
Parking/Tolls							
Other Transportation							
License/Registration							
Car Insurance							
Subscriptions							
Gifts							
Recreation							
Vacation							
Dues/Health Club							
Hair Care/Cosmetics							
Laundry							
Dry Cleaning							
Childcare/School Lunch							
Life Insurance							
Health Insurance							
School							
Alimony/Child Support							
Dental Visits							
Doctor Visits							
Prescriptions/Vitamins							
Clothing							
Installment Payments							
Credit Card Payments							

EXPENSE	WEEK 1	WEEK 2	WEEK 3	WEEK 4	TOTAL	ALLOCATED	COMMENTS
Federal Tax							
State Tax							
Local Tax							
Allowances							
Other							

Tea *Time!*

What can I do to change the "uh-oh!" into "yay!" when it comes to expenditures?

Money and Thee: Finding Your Way

How are you doing so far? Is the book, or your spiral note-book, filled with scribbles and erasure marks, and smiley faces and frowns? Have you scratched out a budget? And are you still among the living? Good! Time to talk about credit.

Now it's your turn to write. Think about what you've read in this chapter. How does it apply to you? Soul-search a little, and jot down your thoughts.

Where I am now: _____

_____

Where I'd like to be: _____

_____

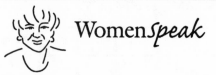 Women*Speak*

"My sixteen-year-old gets credit card offers in the mail all the time. Sometimes I think all you need to get a credit card is a pulse."

————

"My secret for living within my means is to never accumulate credit card debt that I can't pay off monthly in full."

————

"What I know now about money management is that if you can't pay a certain bill, send your creditor anything you can. Once, I got sick and had to go to an emergency clinic. The bill was fairly high, and I could not afford to pay the balance there. Times were tough—my employer lost his business overnight due to alcoholism, leaving me unemployed and without insurance. I sent the clinic $5 per month. After a few months of this, they wrote on my bill '$5 a month is not acceptable.' So I sent them $7 per month until the balance was paid. SOMETHING is better than nothing."

four

It Should Be Called Debit:
The Very Big Business of Credit

Sheila wanted a mountain bike. She was convinced that the bike would bring her untold pleasure. Besides, what could be a better way to lose some weight? The bike she wanted cost $1,000. Sheila reasoned she could pay for the bike with her first-ever credit card, and get extra baby-sitting jobs to augment her part-time work at the college where she studied. Sure, the credit card charged 18 percent interest, but she could make the monthly $20 payments, and besides, the clerk in the store told her the bike was a steal.

As such things go, it didn't work out as planned. For one thing, mountain biking was more strenuous than Sheila had thought. For another, she was surprised to learn about the cost of maintenance. Then the bike was stolen. To top it off, the college cut her hours in half, and baby-sitting was out of the question, considering her study load.

Let's take a close look at Sheila's predicament. How much of her monthly installments went to paying on the bike itself? Since her interest rate was 18 percent, $15 of Sheila's first payment went to interest, $5 went to repayment of the loan. It will take Sheila nearly eight years to repay this loan if she continues to make minimum payments. The bike is long gone. Do you think she will face any other needs or wants in the next eight years? To boot, her credit was hurt because of a poor payment record.

Sheila used easy credit … and needed her bike helmet when reality came crashing down on her with a hard jolt. If Sheila had been informed and fully cognizant of the interest factor, and the terms that came attached to her easy credit, she might have taken up jogging instead!

What You Need to Know About Credit But Were Afraid to Ask

What is credit? Credit is a loan. It is borrowing money you will have to pay back (with interest) from future earnings. Most people take advantage of credit to buy "stuff." Credit, like money, is not a bad thing. Credit *abuse* gets us into trouble.

Why do we have credit? What, if anything, is good about credit? Our society operates on the certainty of credit, and it is through the power of plastic that you are able to negotiate business with many vendors. Credit drives the economy. Many argue that credit is a positive influence in the following ways:

- Improves people's standard of living
- Enables the consumer to take advantage of a good deal or sale
- Makes it possible to purchase "big-ticket" items
- Makes purchases more convenient
- Enables us to better manage finances
- Helps us to establish a favorable credit rating
- Helps us to cope with financial emergencies
- Helps us to keep savings intact

Tea *Time!*

Round up all your credit cards and build a house of cards with them. Even if you have only two cards, balance them on end against each other. When your house of cards falls down, let it lie in a heap while you read on.

The Hard Jolt of Truth

Before you decide to keep your credit cards after all, read on. I'd like to show you the truth behind all the arguments for credit.

Credit improves one's standard of living. Yes, it may. For those who are brilliant at managing payments and factoring *all* the costs of credit use to their advantage, credit enhances their standard of living. Credit makes just about every want immediately attainable. While this may sound desirable, for many this has been the cause of diminishing, rather than improving, their standard of living, as credit card debt creates despair and stress.

Tea *Time!*

Would I go to a bank to borrow several hundred dollars to buy Christmas gifts?

Am I not doing the same thing (at higher interest) when I use my credit cards to fund the holidays?

Credit enables the consumer to take advantage of a good deal or sale. Quite true. But read this true story. Ellen was in a faraway town that boasted of its factory outlet mall. Unable to resist, Ellen went for a look-see, determined not to spend one red cent. The merchandise selection was far greater than anything Ellen had ever seen back home. She was dazzled by the astonishing assortment of goods. It made Shoptilyoudrop & Co. look like the corner mini-mart. And, after all, everything was on sale. Ellen did buy some fine things. Only one "oops!" to this story: Ellen's credit card has a 19 percent interest rate, *and* since she had an existing balance, the interest on the new purchases began that very day. Overall, Ellen saved 20 percent on her collective purchase. Let's do a little math. If she paid her credit card bill in full (which she did not, opting for installments), Ellen "saved" 1 percent on merchandise she was quite content to be without, until she fell prey to the lure of the outlet mall. Since Ellen didn't pay her bill in full, the 1 percent savings will be long gone, absorbed by the choke-hold of her credit card interest. Some sale.

Credit makes it possible to purchase big-ticket items. This may or may not be a valid argument. Let's look at the big-ticket items in most homes. The first thing we think of is the home itself. Home purchase, however, is normally considered an investment because of equity. Next, we think of cars. Once again, *if financed at or below resale value,* it may be considered an investment because of equity. Many people owe more on their cars than the car is worth—not an equity situation! (More on homes and cars in chapter eleven.) Appliances are certainly big-ticket items. Some appliance stores offer special deals for installment purchase—so many days the same as cash, no interest for the first year, low interest. If you've shopped for an item, a refrigerator for example, and the price is consistent with fair market value, it may be worth paying a little interest to enjoy the benefit of refrigeration now. There are certainly times when credit, if used wisely, can work for you. (Milk sours awfully fast at room temperature.)

On the other hand, resorting to interest and installments just because you got bored with your avocado fridge (that still keeps your milk nice and cold!) might be a *mis*-use of credit!

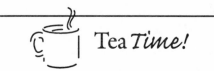 Tea *Time!*

If you justify buying the expensive sound system by insisting you can "handle" $100 monthly payments, why on earth can't you put the $100 in savings each month and stick with the old boom box until you can pay for your new sound system with cash?

Credit makes purchases more convenient. No question, some things are easier to do (or purchase) when you use credit: catalogue goods, motels, rental cars, just to name a few. And it's quicker than producing your driver's license (and often two credit cards) to validate your check.

Time for a parable. Just yesterday, Joe and I headed to a town twenty-five miles away. As we were leaving our village, a car came up from behind and glued itself to our bumper. Joe pulled aside to let the hurried young woman pass, and we tootled on our way. Want to make a guess whose bumper we pulled up behind when we approached the first stoplight in the next town?

What difference does it make if you take *one more minute* to write a check? If you are in such a big hurry, pay with cash. Or use a debit card. Debit cards have all the appearance of credit cards with one BIG difference: When the plastic card is run through the store's computer, the cost of your purchase is automatically deducted from your bank account.

Credit enables people to better manage finances. Yes, some people are efficient and systematic, and pay everything in full or on time. So, having the credit card bill simplifies matters. As does a consolidation loan. But this point is only valid in those cases where individuals keep track of their spending and pay off their credit card balance each month.

Credit helps establish a favorable credit rating. Absolutely, positively, yes—unless you miss a few payments now and then. If you are the kind of person who pays off the balance on your credit card each month, credit cards may be a way for you to get credit. As you will soon read, creditors put your income and your bill-paying history under a microscope when you apply for a loan. Unless you are certain you will never apply for a mortgage, or any kind of loan *ever*, you need a good credit history. More on this later.

Credit helps us to cope with financial emergency. True. More than one person has suddenly had to take a flight because of a medical or family emergency. At a time of stress, the convenience of credit is handy. Your best bet, though, is to have an emergency fund for such occurrences.

Credit helps us keep our savings intact. Yes and no. Once again, this depends on your overall ability to manage money. If your savings are collecting a higher interest under a CD, for instance, and you'd face interest penalties for withdrawing before maturity, it might be better to go with a small loan. Credit cards rarely qualify as a substitute, unless they carry a low interest rate.

Mark this down: **When you use a credit card or borrow funds, you are not spending *your* money, you are spending someone else's!** Here are the hard, cold facts about credit:

- Credit is a loan. It is your future income already spent. Kaput.
- Credit provides false security. Plastic in your hand gives you a feeling of power and control. You can do anything, have your heart's desire. If that's what you think, look again at the heap of credit cards on the table. *That* is your security.
- Conservative statistics tell us that many Americans are up to their limit on credit. Twenty percent or more of their monthly income goes to debt reduction.
- Credit holds "hidden" costs. Finance charges and interest add substantially to the cost of your purchase, as do late payment (and with some companies, early payment) penalties.
- Abuse of credit can destroy your creditworthiness, and actually lead to loss of what you already have. Just ask Sarah. Her story is extreme, but true.

Sarah was in a heap of trouble. On her own, with two children, after her husband, John, walked out, she amassed crippling debt on her credit cards. Instead of asking for help, she kept her financial problems to herself.

At first, Sarah's teaching salary, combined with child support, was adequate. Initially, child support went to pay the mortgage, then to credit installments, until ultimately (because she was totally out of control), Sarah simply spent the money recklessly.

Her debt began to mount as she started using her charge card for everything—her groceries, her gas. She felt sorry for her kids, so she outfitted them with new wardrobes. In a few months, the collectors started to call. She left incoming phone calls to the answering machine and hid any mail that looked like a bill (or a threat) in a box in the basement. She even tried to hide from the sheriff when he came to deliver her foreclosure notice, since her mortgage hadn't been paid in months.

Sarah was utterly despondent. The paralysis of her fear kept her from facing her spending problems and dealing with them. In the end she lost everything. John was awarded temporary custody of the children until she demonstrated that she had stopped her destructive behavior.

Though Sarah's story is an extreme case, financial counselors nod their heads in sad confirmation, and tell me that unless destructive behavior is changed, many others are following in her footprints. She is now in counseling and working hard to overcome her addiction to spending. For Sarah—and for many people—easy credit is far too easy to abuse.

You may not have a compulsive need to spend, and you may be responsible enough to handle credit. If so, for you, the good aspects of credit far outweigh the negatives.

Should You Have a Credit Card?

Now that I've warned you of the evils of credit card abuse, I will say that I believe it's wise to have one credit card. From everything I have learned, it is imperative that a woman have credit *in her name.* If you don't trust yourself to be responsible in the use of your credit card, do what one financial counselor recommends: freeze it in a mayonnaise jar filled with water. The narrow neck of the jar, along with the fact that you can't microwave it because of the metal strip on the back of your card, gives you a "cooling off" period.

When used responsibly, credit cards are an advantage. Just be careful. The credit business is highly profitable for the issuing card company, *as long as you stay in debt.* The combination of interest, cash advance charges, and other fees gives the credit-card issuers billions of dollars of profit each year. Billions of *your* dollars, I might add. Seductive offers come by mail, and offer to ease your credit crunch by promising lower introductory interest rates. But the fine print contains clauses that would curl your toes.

Don't forget: *Credit card accounts are designed to keep you in debt forever ... that's how they make their money and stay in business.*

 Tea *Time!*

Before you use your credit card to purchase something, ask yourself, "Is this charge I'm making worth losing my freedom by going into debt and financial bondage?"

Do some research to determine the best credit card to have. Consumer magazines often dedicate an issue to the status of credit, and credit cards, in our country. Go to your library and ask the research desk to help you find a recent issue that evaluates all the cards offered, and also publishes names of banks and firms that offer the best deals.

Check with the bank or credit union you do business with. Tell them you are shopping. Bankcard Holders of America will send you a printout of the best bets for credit cards. (Call directory assistance at 1-800-555-1212 to obtain their current 800 number.) Universities, clubs, organizations—even catalogue companies—offer their own cards.

Here are two rules about the type of credit card you should have:

1. *No annual fee.* There is only one reason you should be paying an annual fee on credit cards these days, and that is if you have a co-branded credit card. Otherwise, you should not have to pay an annual fee. The competition for your dollar is too great. If you are paying a fee, call your company and announce you would like the card for free.

Co-branded cards are relatively new in the credit industry and may be a sensible consideration, provided there are not high annual fees or high interest. Under a co-branded system, credit card firms team up with car makers, airlines, and other businesses to offer rebates or incentives (frequent flier miles, money off on the next car) to card users. Many cardholders use the card for the express purpose of benefiting from the arrangement. Co-branded cards usually charge an annual fee.

2. *A low interest rate.* If you have a high rate now, call your company and tell them you want a lower rate. If they say no, ask to speak to a manager. If you still get a no, wait a day and call again (you will get another person). If you can't get a lower rate, find another card company. Of course, if you follow the advice of this book, card interest rates will be unimportant, since you are paying your bill in full each month!

Note: Most store credit cards are not recommended, for two reasons. First, they usually charge the highest interest rates. Second, they don't offer broad usage. (OK, OK, so they offer you "instant credit" and give you a free box of chocolates when you sign up ... hmmm, maybe worth reconsidering.) Whimsy aside, this *may* be a logical approach to establishing good credit. It may also be a trapdoor, as it encourages you to develop your "charging" skills. And remember those very high interest penalties!

If you have never had a credit card before, you may be turned down unless you've established a good credit history. You may have established good credit without intending to. For example, if you took out a student loan and have been prompt in your payments, you may be considered creditworthy. One of the most certain ways to build good credit, I am told, is to repay your student loan promptly. This kind of character and responsibility scores big points with lenders. You can check with a credit bureau to see if you have a credit history, or to see how solid it is (see page 98).

How Can You Establish a Credit History If You Don't Have One?

If you have never taken out a loan or had a credit card in your name, you probably don't have a credit history. If that's the case, you need to establish history right away. Here are two ways to establish your creditworthiness.

Take out a small loan from a bank. To do this, you must establish a rock-solid relationship with a good bank. Maintain a minimum balance in your checking account (never accidentally overdraft). Start a savings account that shows regular deposits, even if the amounts are small.

Once you have a good record at your bank, apply for a small loan. Some banks still have loan officers. (Loan officers are becoming an endangered species; many banks now have automated loan departments. Your application is evaluated, and approved or disapproved, according to a preset formula.) Try to communicate that you are attempting to establish creditworthiness, and want the loan to be unsecured (without collateral or co-signature). *Do not spend this money on anything.*

When you get the loan, walk it over to the teller and deposit it in savings or a money market account. Be certain your loan payments are on time, and pay the loan off early. The little bit of interest you pay is worth the good reputation you are building.

Buy something "on time" from a store that extends credit through installment payments. If you choose this option, be sure you know what you're doing when you sign the contract. Pay faithfully, don't be late, and try to pay the full amount earlier than the contract stipulates.

A variation on this point is to pay doctor and other medical bills through extended credit.

If you are offered a credit card, and have carefully considered the grave responsibility attached to owning one, go ahead, pay off all charges at the end of each month, and establish your credit history that way.

Getting the Lowdown on Interest Rates

Credit is big business. Credit card companies and banks will do what they can to lure you to use their cards. The quickest way to get your business is to hook you with the promise of payoff. Here's how it works: Jeannette gets in over her head with one company and doesn't know where to turn. Then a "miracle" occurs. The mailman brings an offer for low interest (for six months, after which the APR jumps sky high!) and, lo and behold, Jeannette can transfer her balance from that nasty company that is causing her sleepless nights. She is positive she will be able to get out from under this debt if she just gets some breathing room. She is certain she won't use those cards again. Jeannette needs relief, so she switches.

May I be a little brazen here? Jeannette is not living in the real world, and neither are you, if this is the way you think. All this scenario does is prolong the inevitable—at a cost, no less. (Remember Sheila and her bicycle?)

Interest is the fee charged by a lender, for lending money. Interest is why some people buy a house for $100,000 and end up paying $250,000 by the time the mortgage is retired. Interest is a bogeyman, but without charging interest, lenders would not lend money, and they would not be in business, and there would be no credit.

The Annual Percentage Rate (APR) is how much interest your credit card company charges you. But many cards calculate interest based on the "effective rate," which is the rate after they factor in finance charges. What does that mean to you? That if you even *know* how much interest you are paying, you may be paying up to a percentage point *more* than what you think. In other words, if you think you are paying 18 percent interest, you'd better check your bill; in many cases 18 percent really means 19.56 percent.

Credit card companies charge you higher interest rates for loaning you money than other institutions. So do *not* borrow money on your credit card. Not only is a cash advance usually billed *at an even higher interest rate*, it often carries a fee of up to 4 percent, which is added to the balance of what you owe. Ouch.

Tea *Time!*

Repeat after me: High interest and low monthly payments will keep me in debt for a long, long time. Low interest and higher payments will free me.

Which do I choose?

Money and Thee: Finding Your Way

Now that you are a bit more informed about the way credit works, just how do you get a loan, and where do you go? If you're a bit intimidated by all of this information, then I've done my job! Too many of us (myself included) have for too long taken our credit fitness for granted. So few of us take the time or effort to become informed, in order to make sound choices. You, however, have chosen to take control of your finances—or you wouldn't be reading this book!

Now it's your turn to write. Think about what you have read in this chapter. How does it apply to you? Soul-search a little, and jot down your thoughts.

Where I am now: _____

_____

_____

Where I'd like to be: _____

_____

_____

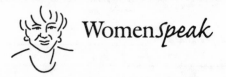

Women*Speak*

"I've negotiated for a couple of rather large loans for our business. This may just be my experience, but I have found women bankers much more respectful of my potential and enterprise than men. One guy—the president of the bank, no less—treated me like a bimbo. I walked out. That bank lost a big account when I left."

———

"I ended up having a lien filed against me because I cosigned a loan with my husband—and he's the one who skipped town!"

———

"You read the papers and get the impression that everyone's declaring bankruptcy, and it's a piece of cake. Well, take it from me, it isn't. We have suffered over and over again because of our bankruptcy. Like right now, we really need another car, but we can't get credit."

———

"I had the screaming baby in one hand, the dog's collar in another, and when I got the door open there was this strange man from the collection agency. I had absolutely no idea what he was talking about. My husband hadn't made a payment on the mobile home in months. We would have lost it if my parents hadn't come to our rescue."

five

Hey, Sister, Can You Loan Me a Dime?

As some of us have learned along the way, it is often a lot easier to borrow than to pay back! The central theme of this chapter is borrowing and "returning," with emphasis on establishing and protecting creditworthiness. This chapter will offer advice to help you get the loan you need, encourage you to maintain a sterling credit reputation, and (I hope!) lend you a snorkel in case you're drowning in a financial pickle barrel! And because a book about money would be incomplete without it, we will discuss the tragedy of bankruptcy—a far cry from your intent when you first acquired a loan!

So let us start at the beginning. Just how *do* you go about getting that loan in the first place?

Loan Application 101

To acquire a loan, you usually must provide your credit history. To provide your credit history, you often need to take out a loan! This is the proverbial "chicken or the egg" scenario. Since I figure we need to have the chicken before we can develop our (ahem) "nest" egg, here is some general information to know about applying for a loan:

Whether you are applying for a credit card or a loan, you are asking someone to lend you money. The lender wants to know about your character, your income, and your creditworthiness.

Character. The lender wants to know that you are reliable—
that you have presented yourself and your situation accurately,
and that you will follow through on your agreement to pay
back the loan. How do you present yourself? Are you well
groomed? Is your outlook positive, your handshake firm? What
is your attitude toward this loan? Do you act as if it is owed to
you? Do you have a personal history of deceit or thievery? Is
your need for money realistic? (If this is a first-time loan, the
bank may be hesitant to lend you money to go to Tahiti for the
weekend.) Where do you live? Have you moved often (and
therefore, are you a bit unsettled)? Do you rent, or own your
own home?

Creditworthiness. The loan officer will also assess your creditworthiness. Are you a good risk? Can you repay the loan? What
is your work experience? What do you do, how long have you
worked at your present job, and what are your qualifications?
How many different jobs have you held, and for how long did
you hold each one?

If you don't work, the lender will be curious about how you
intend to pay back a loan. Be prepared to give an answer. You
could be as straightforward as this: "My husband is the primary
breadwinner in our home. If you check, you will see that our
joint credit history is impeccable. My purpose with this loan is
to establish credit in my name only." This may not be necessary
if you are already establishing creditworthiness by sharing an
account with your husband.

The lending institution will also be entitled to know how
much money you make.

Do you have a checking or savings account, certificates of
deposit, or investments of any kind? Do you have equity in a

home, a car, or land? What is your current indebtedness? How do you intend to pay back this loan? Have you ever been in default of a loan, or declared bankruptcy, or do you have a history of consistent late payment?

Loans can be varied and made-to-order. You will impress the lending officer if you know what kind of loan you are asking for. "Um...I need some money to go to Tahiti for a week" might fly if you said, instead, "I am interested in a short-term note for personal improvement."

Installment or consumer loans. An installment, or consumer, loan is simply a loan to get money to buy or fix something. It can be for payment of a specific item (a car) and for a specific time (four years). An installment loan can also be for cash (for example, to pay for a wedding).

Short-term loan: This is when the amount borrowed, plus interest, is payable at the end of a short term, such as 120 days.

Mortgage, Veteran's Administration (VA), and Federal Housing Administration (FHA) loans: These home-buying loans will be covered in detail in chapter eleven.

Passbook loan. If you have money in savings, you can make a "passbook loan," which is borrowing up to the amount you have in savings, using savings as collateral. But this doesn't usually make sense—*most savings accounts earn less interest than you would pay on a loan.* If it's an important purchase, and if you're not touching your emergency fund, use the money from savings.

Secured or unsecured loans: If you have collateral (land, home, car), then you can "guarantee" your loan repayment by allowing the bank to put a lien on your property until the loan is satisfied. This is called a *secured* loan, which in one sense is not a loan at all, since the bank will be paid with *something*, even if you default. An *unsecured* loan is one that is extended to you without collateral.

Interest can vary substantially, so be sure to shop around to determine the best rates available. I also recommend that you ask if there are prepayment penalties attached to the loan—a penalty assessed if you pay off the loan sooner than the contract stipulates. Many unregulated finance companies charge prepayment penalties in the form of *full term interest due*. In other words, your loan contract might stipulate X amount of dollars for five years, plus interest. If you pay off the loan in two years, the full five years' worth of interest is due. If you run into this situation, go someplace else! Banks, because they are regulated, will rarely charge a penalty.

So, where do you go when you want money?

Pardon Me, I'd Like to Take Out a Loan

If you need a loan, you can turn to several places: banks, savings and loans, credit unions, insurance companies, and finance companies.

Banks, savings and loans. Should you go to your bank for a loan? Well...probably. *Hey,* you're saying, *I thought you told us to develop creditworthiness with our own bank.* Yes, and that will help you with a loan *any*where, not just with your bank. It certainly is good business to stick with one place and establish a sterling reputation. That way, if an emergency arises, much of the hassle (and anxiety over approval) is gone. Banks, however, vary as to interest rates or loan activation fees, closing costs, and so on, so shop for the best rates. Banks are regulated by government agencies, and they offer a creative variety of loans, as well as revolving lines of credit.

Credit unions. If you belong to a credit union, you may have to look no further for a loan. Credit unions are nonprofit associations, created for and by people who have employment or some other association in common. For instance, as a federal employee, my husband belongs to the Government Employees Federal Credit Union.

Insurance companies. Borrowing from the cash value on a life insurance policy can make a lot of sense. Interest rates are usually low, compared to other lending institutions, and you have the option of not repaying the loan, which, along with interest, will be deducted from either death benefits or the surrender value of the policy.

Finance companies. This may be your only resort if you have bad credit, but try to stay clear of these places. The interest will eat you alive.

It is possible—though not probable—that the lending institution does not fulfill its obligation *to you.* If that happens, there are several laws that protect you from sloppy or illegal behavior by the lender.

It's the Law

You are protected by law when it comes to credit transactions. Here is an overview of the consumer credit laws in our country.

Truth in Lending Act. Anyone lending you money must give you accurate and full credit costs and terms at onset of a loan.

Equal Credit Opportunity Act. You may not be discriminated against *based on* your age, sex, marital status, reliance on income from public assistance, race, color, religion, or national origin. However, if you have poor credit history or cannot show character or the ability to repay, the lender may deny credit.

Fair Debt Collection Practices Act. This law applies to the people in the collection agency, who are hired by the lenders to get their money.
- The collection agent may not use abusive language.
- Phone calls must be after 8:00 A.M. and before 9:00 P.M. Excessive calls are outlawed.
- Threats to notify employers or friends of your delinquency is against the law.
- Using false pretense to gain entry to your home for repossession is illegal.
- Trying to collect more than the debt is illegal.
- Sending you misleading mail is against the law.

Fair Credit Billing Act. This allows consumers to correct mistakes on their credit card accounts in a speedy manner.

What if you are turned down for a loan? Can you do anything? Perhaps. Let me explain.

What Happens If You Are Turned Down for a Loan?

Maybe a credit bureau has sent an unfavorable report about you to your lender. A credit bureau is in the business to know your business. They collect everything they can about your credit behavior, and provide this information to qualified businesses that pay them a fee. If your credit rating is A plus, the credit bureau will report that to the inquiring agency. If it is a big fat zero, they will report that as well. Some credit bureaus are privately owned, some are nonprofit, some specialize in mortgage reporting. They obtain their information from stores, banks, public records, employers, and collection agencies.

What exactly do they report?

- All pertinent personal data about you: name, changes of names, age, Social Security number, addresses, employers, what you do for a living, information on your husband, whether you rent or own
- All data from all loans: date, amount, terms
- May have information about times you *attempted* to obtain credit
- Credit history: Your file is often updated to show outstanding balances, past-due amounts, whether you consistently pay late
- Maximum credit limits on your credit cards
- Bankruptcies, lawsuits, judgments, liens, repossessions, wage garnishments

Yikes. How long does that stuff stay on there? Seven years on average; up to ten for bankruptcy.

Tea *Time!*

Call your credit bureau (ask your lending agency or bank which one they use) and ask for a copy of the data on you. Expect to be charged a fee. Don't forget, if you are denied a loan, you may request a free copy of your report for up to thirty days.

There are three major credit bureaus in the United States: Equifax Credit Information Services, Experian, and Trans Union Corporation: Call 1-800-555-1212 for their current 800 numbers.

If you are turned down for a loan, find out *why* you were denied credit. You are entitled to a free copy of your credit report. Go over the report with a magnifying glass. Check the information for accuracy. If there is a disputed item, you are entitled by law to write a reason for the blip on your report, which must be attached to your file.

If there is a dispute, you have the right to complete a dispute form and send it to the credit bureau. Allow them a few weeks to correct their records, and check with them again. Bottom line: If you are denied a loan for a valid reason, you have to bite the bullet and strive toward proving your creditworthiness.

Suppose you have absolutely no creditworthiness—zip—and are so down-and-out that a loan, or an extension of credit, is no longer an option. What do you do if you are thinking of bankruptcy?

Where to Go for Help If You're in a Financial Pickle Barrel

If you think I'm talking nonsense when I tell you to turn to Jesus Christ, then you haven't been paying attention. Prayer is the surest way to give you the courage, the strength, the conviction, and the power to face your situation if you are in a bind.

I've said this before, but it bears repeating, go to your church, *especially* if you are a single mom or widowed. Many, many churches have members who volunteer their services and can guide you through these troubled waters.

Look in the phone book for a listing for Consumer Credit Counseling Services. There are over seven hundred of these not-for-profit agencies in the United States. If you can't find a local listing, call the 1-800-555-1212 directory assistance line.

Besides the help offered in these pages, Larry Burkett, Ron Blue, and others have written books on money that offer you a self-guided tour through the credit maze. Go to the library and check out one of these books.

Collection Agencies

Sometimes, you will get help from the very people who are hired to wring that last drop of blood out of your checking account. Many collection agencies, for instance, will work with you if you demonstrate a willing spirit.

I cannot stress this enough: Creditors do not want to repossess your car or your house or your TV; they don't want to cause you stress, nor do they want to sue you. They just want their money. If you are having a hard time financially, *commu-*

nicate with your creditors. You may be able to work out a solution with them.

A good friend of mine works for a collection agency. I sat face-to-face with him on your behalf. He pointedly repeated that the very best way out of your dilemma is to have a willing spirit, and to try to work out an acceptable payment plan with the creditor.

There is a myth, however, that most creditors will accept as little as one dollar each month, regardless of the amount owed. This payment supposedly reflects your intent to pay. Many creditors will not accept such a small amount and will hold you to a minimum payment. Do what you can to meet your obligations.

If, for some reason, you find yourself face-to-face with a collection agent, there are a few things you should know:

- The worst thing you can do is to ignore a collection agency.
- Most agencies will work with you if you are honest about what you can pay (as long as it is within reason).
- Some agencies will work with their client, who has hired them to collect the debt. For example, if you owe medical bills to a hospital, the collection agent may get the hospital to "settle" with a reduced bill.
- Collection agencies will usually give you thirty days notice of default before they're repossess something. They will factor in past performance to determine how much slack they will give you.
- If something is repossessed, a ten-day notice of redemption will be offered. You may be liable for extra expenses after repossession, though, such as repairs or moving fees. If you refuse to vacate the premises, a "replevin" action

can be taken against you. In this case the collection agency turns your account over to an attorney, who goes to the police, who serve a "show cause" order why you shouldn't move out of your home. You then have forty-eight hours to get out. If you don't go, the police will come and escort you.

Credit Clinics

Not all credit clinics are created equal. If you go to a clinic that promises to fix your poor credit rating, you may be paying for something you can do yourself. Credit clinics often charge exorbitant rates for services. They do this because you are desperate. You can dispute information in your credit bureau file, all by yourself, and save the fee. If your bad credit history information is correct, no one but the creditor can make a change, anyway. If you have bad credit, follow the suggestions in this book, or other books, to build it back up.

Declaring Bankruptcy

What if, as discussed a little earlier, your credit is kaput? What if you've done everything humanly (and spiritually) possible, and there is simply no way out of that pickle barrel?

Bankruptcy is a last resort. Those who treat it cavalierly and sell you on going into bankruptcy as an easy answer to your financial problems are not looking after your best interest. It is an answer to some of your problems. But it is not an easy answer. It contains long-term negative consequences that can affect all aspects of your life for years to come.[1]

Bankruptcy is a real blot on your creditworthiness. Sadly, some women go along for the ride when a spouse files bankruptcy. It may take some lengthy visits to the bank, and a few written disclaimers attached to your credit file, to pull yourself away from this unfortunate last resort.

Should you declare bankruptcy? Is it even Christian to do so? Good question. It may be time for a reminder that how we handle everything in life—including debt—reflects on Jesus. This is no small thing. You may have to consider bankruptcy for the following reasons:

- You have no other option.
- You have sought the counsel of professionals, and it is their opinion this is necessary.
- You will try to repay your debt when you are solvent.

There are two main types of bankruptcy: Chapter 7 and Chapter 13.

Chapter 7. Under this type of bankruptcy, everything you own that is not exempt by law (check your state laws) is turned over to the court, which then liquidates your assets to pay creditors. Once a creditor is notified that you are filing Chapter 7, they may not contact you for payment.

Chapter 13. Under this type of bankruptcy, your creditors are notified they can't continue any legal action against you, but you must work out a plan to pay them back. Chapter 13 does not relieve you of debt; it takes the heat off.

What You Still Owe

Bankruptcy does not discharge you from all debt. Obligations that cannot be eliminated by filing bankruptcy are:

- any taxes due the IRS
- alimony and child support
- guaranteed student loans
- liabilities created by fraudulent action

- liabilities resulting from theft and/or destruction of private property
- debt not reported on bankruptcy forms, or debts for which the creditor's name and address were incorrectly listed

Bailing Out of Bankruptcy
You are not the first woman to find herself at the end of her rope. For whatever reason, bankruptcy has become part of your credit history. Most likely, you are now alone, and determined to start fresh. What can you do?

Continue to seek help. Bankruptcy stays on your credit record for ten years. Agencies such as Consumer Credit Counseling Service will advise you on what steps to take to bring vibrancy and health back to your creditworthiness.

You may be able to obtain a loan, regardless of bankruptcy, by following the principles already outlined, talking personally with the banker, and demonstrating your sincerity. Also, some loan companies offer loans to people who have experienced bankruptcy (usually at extremely high interest rates).

The important thing for you to remember is that other women have walked in your shoes. Many people—probably *most* people—have at one time or another found themselves desperate because of their financial condition. Whether they were responsible for their predicament or not, their pillows were wet from tears shed over this utterly frightening issue. Many of those women are smiling now.

Money and Thee: Finding Your Way

Try to keep your money problems in perspective, keep your knees bent in prayer, your eyes focused on the hem of heaven, and bolster yourself with the assurance that you will smile again. See? I can see a little smile already!

We're going to turn our attention, in the next chapter, to how some of us have found ourselves in the pickle barrel with a sprig of dill jutting off the tips of our noses!

But now it's your turn to write. Think about what you have read in this chapter. How does it apply to you? Soul-search a little, and jot down your thoughts.

Where I am now: _____

_____

_____

Where I'd like to be: _____

_____

_____

Women *speak*

"Watch impulse buying. Listen to your conscience when shopping. If you feel a tug in your gut—even a little tug—don't buy it. A couple days later, you won't even notice you don't have the item ... if you can even remember what it was."

———

"If a parent is self-absorbed, lazy, or forced by economic pressure to be absent, then a family often falls apart."

———

"My husband didn't have a grasp on what our financial situation was until he began balancing our checkbook about six months ago. Since then, he's been much more understanding about why I say no to his clotheshorse impulses, and he understands that the reason I'm not impulsive is not that I'm uptight, but that it wouldn't be a wise use of our resources."

———

"I was fortunate to have a mother who learned the hard way how to hold on to money, but extended the grace to teach me, before I had to suffer any unnecessary scrapes and bruises. The most important thing she did for me was to take me to the bank as soon as I started making money—probably from baby-sitting during my junior high years. She showed me how to make deposits and withdrawals, how to record interest earned on my account, and eventually how to invest in a CD. Before I took off for college, she helped me open a checking account, showed me how to balance my checkbook from the statements, and clued me in on how much more expensive it is to order checks from the bank (highway robbery) than from a mail-order service."

six

Love and Money:
A Look at You, Hubby, and the Kids

All the writing experts say the same thing—don't be negative, don't scare people, don't make them feel guilty. I say phooey. Some things need to be said, so grin and bear with me! I promise not to stay negative throughout this entire chapter, which aims to take a peek at how we love, abuse, or master money, and how our actions relate to other family members. Ready? Here goes.

Somebody's got to say it. *Americans are drunk with consumer glut.* We have been conditioned through millions of commercials, magazine ads, and consumer come-ons to spend money on anything that appeals to our senses or brings a moment's stimulation or joy. Our lives are shaped by advertising. Christians, too, have become unsettled and restless.

Short of homesteading in the Yukon, it is impossible to escape our consumer culture. But is consumerism consistent with Christian virtue? Certainly we must consume just to live in our world, but we have become irresponsible, and sometimes greedy, spenders. We don't worry about the consequences until they catch up with our reckless spending behavior. We are all guilty.

Tea *Time!*

Think I'm too severe? Stop for a moment and look around your house. Find one object you recently purchased that you "had to have." Just one. Now ask yourself these questions: Did having that item change my life in some significant way? Could I have sailed along without it? How long did it interest me? How much money did I spend on it?

Money Is a State of Mind

You may need to change the way you think about, and handle, money. If you are upbeat, and determined to manage money wisely, you will begin to live that way. Once you develop the habit of saying no to impulse buying, pay off all those bills, and shop frugally, the rest will take care of itself.

When I was in the insurance business, a man quite a few years my senior gave me sage advice: "Cynthia," he said, "take care of your clients, and the commission will take care of itself." I've applied that principle to many things over the years, and I can apply it here: Take care of the day-to-day spending habits, and you will be surprised how much is left over to save.

Bold as I am to point an accusatory finger, I am aware that many things, including my diatribe about our spending glut, are easier said than fixed. "You may need to change the way you think about and handle money," is a statement that applies differently to each and every one of us, because we are all different.

Tell my husband and me to walk across the street, and we will each take our own route to the same lamppost. Not too many people think the same way. That is one reason we rejoice when we make a friend who turns out to be a "kindred spirit."

I've put together a list of possible shopping personalities, hoping that you can laugh a little while you think about your state of mind when it comes to money. (See? I promised I wouldn't stay grumpy!) Let's look at the spenders first.

Happy-Go-Lucky Lil. Lil loves life. In fact, she loves life so much that unless she's having F-U-N, it's been a bad day. Lil laughs a lot, is impetuous, and commands attention. She doesn't sweat the details, like who is going to pay for all the fun. As long as Lil has cash flow, the rainy days will have to wait. Besides, it doesn't rain in Lil's world.

Bertha Binge. Bertha rewards herself with shopping sprees, because she's been so good—and, after all, it's been so-o-o-o long since she bought something. All purchases, whether expensive steak for dinner or a new summer dress, are justified when Bertha binges.

Shop-Till-You-Drop Suzy. Suzy should not leave home (or turn on the shopping channel) without a bodyguard. It is Suzy's manifest destiny to shop. She is an authority on bargains and store layouts, knows all the clerks on a first-name basis, and gets an adrenaline rush when she steps inside a mall. An outlet store? Pure ecstasy.

Generous Gertie. Gertie justifies her consumer frenzy by shopping for others. It's a done deal: Gertie satisfies her need to shop, has a ball, and lavishes friends and family with gifts. People like to see Gertie at their door.

Vindictive Vicky: Vicky brings new meaning to the expression "I don't get mad, I get even." She gets mad *and* even. If her husband steps out of line, she writes checks and uses the charge card to "show him" a thing or two. What a mess.

Frugal Fran. Fran learned a long time ago that frugal means smart, not fanatic. She follows her budget with diligence (and occasional slips) and shops wisely. Fran, like Suzy, is aware of a good sale. She will not spend money for the "sake of a sale," however, unless she needs something. Fran has learned to be content with her circumstance.

Now let's look at the savers:

The World Is Coming to an End Wanda. If people like to see Gertie at their door, they close the drapes when Wanda heads up the sidewalk. Wanda is a prophetess of doom. She doesn't trust anyone, takes hours convincing others of conspiracies, and exchanges all of her money for gold. Wanda is saving for Armageddon, as if she would have *use* for her money when that time comes.

Pack-Rat Roberta. Roberta saves...everything. Her house is filled with boxes and boxes of stuff. There's probably money in that clutter, somewhere. Roberta doesn't shop as much as she "collects."

Marilyn the Martyr. Poor Marilyn. She's a saint. She goes

without, just so others can get ahead. Her son will get to college even if she has to scrub floors for a living. Her daughter can go on the class trip because Roberta will just delay getting that cavity filled. After all, there's always aspirin.

A Joyless Scrooge Called Shirley. Shirley is working toward her Ph.D. in saving. She's tighter than the rubber band on her broccoli. "Skinflint" and "cheapskate" are labels she accepts proudly. She reasons her way out of any purchase, and everyone else's purchase, as well, and shoots cold glances to make others feel guilty. Shirley is no joy to be around.

Sensible Sandra. Like the woman in Proverbs 31, Sandra can laugh at times to come, because she is prepared. Sandra has saved *something* since she was a child (thanks to the guidance of sensible parents), and at thirty-three, she hasn't skipped a beat. Sandra and her family live within their means, and have money in savings. Her husband "has full confidence in her and lacks nothing of value" (Proverbs 31:11).

Tea *Time!*

Which woman are you?

I've been a little blunt, and we've laughed a little, yet for some of you reading this book, the tragedy of your inability to control spending or manage money is no laughing matter. You are utterly frozen with guilt and fear over the mess you're in. As mentioned in an earlier chapter, you must turn to God and seek his help, and the help of others. For some of you, there is a huge hurdle to face—telling your husband. Some of you must first apprise your husband of the true state of the household finances. This must be a horrible burden for you to bear. I pray that the advice given here will afford you the courage and incentive to take this important action.

Telling Your Husband the Truth

Margi hated herself for the lies she told her husband, but the deception was easier to live with than the fear that Stan would leave her if he found out. She felt guilty and ashamed, but still spent recklessly. She knew all the lies would catch up with her sooner or later, but she never dreamed that Stan was more devastated by her betrayal than by the debt she'd amassed.

Some women have careened into nightmarish debt and successfully hidden the fact from their husbands. They hide their purchases, lie about acquisition ("I bought this at the thrift store"), and hide the bills. They want help, but they are scared witless to tell their unsuspecting husbands the truth of their predicament. Does that sound like you? Take a deep breath.

You must tell the truth, face his reaction, and begin healing. You must, because this issue is eating you alive. If you are sincere in your determination to change, you have to start the process. Trust God, and ask him to give you and your husband the grace—and the will—to deal with your problem.

Should you expect your husband to react emotionally? Yes. Money is a very emotional issue. It goes to the top of the list as a cause of divorce, and arguments over money push a lot of buttons. In their book *Money Demons*, Susan Forward and Craig Buck write:

Millions of marriages and intimate relationships have been torn apart by money fights. Couples split up over money more often than they do over anything else, including children, sex, and in-laws.[1]

I will add that counselors tell me that women in this situation are often surprised by the understanding reaction from their husbands, so don't despair. The *fear* of reaction from others is usually worse than the reaction.

Don't let the stress of your impending discussion cause you to slip back into denial, then appease the stress by spending more. Consider the following tips before you talk.

1. *Pray before the discussion.* If your husband will not join you in prayer, pray solo. Make a conscious decision not to let this issue take over.

2. *Organize all your bills* as outlined in chapter two. Can some purchases be returned? Can you work out an easier payment schedule? Can you cut back on other expenses until the bills are paid? Most important, are you determined to seek help or counsel to get to the root of this spending problem?

3. *Set a definite appointment for the discussion.* Arrange a time to meet with your husband when both of you will be undisturbed.

4. *Follow the suggestions listed here to help ensure the success of your talk.*

   - Find a private place (behind closed doors).
   - Take the phone off the hook.
   - Tell the kids you are not to be interrupted.
   - Talk face-to-face.
   - Remain as rational as possible; separate all the baggage associated with your money problems: past history,

childhood trauma, and so on.
- Allow each other to vent a little. It's not fair to deny each other expression of emotion, or time to process the conversation.

No one can predict your husband's response, but I can guarantee yours: You will feel relieved of a great weight once you share your secret.

Reckless spending, however, is not always a secret, and as several women have shared with me, it is just as much a *guy* problem as it is a gal's. Some women are married to fellows who can't resist the latest gizmo hawked on TV, a new tool, or the upgraded "big-boy toy," when it hits the market. This can be a tricky problem.

What If Your Husband Can't/Won't Manage Money?

In a fallen world, we sometimes have to cope with our circumstances, and deal with others who might not bear up under responsibility. Perhaps you are not irresponsible in your financial affairs, but your husband is. Or perhaps you are married to a man who will not share one iota of information with you about money affairs, and though he provides well, leaves you in the dark.

According to Susan Forward and Craig Buck, who devote a lengthy chapter on money-reckless men in theirr book *Money Demons*, men who are reckless with money are a bigger threat to financial stability than are women with the same problem. Their reasoning is straightforward: Women, they maintain, usually *know* they are out of control. Men, on the other hand, rarely own up to wrong behavior, and even more rarely will try to do anything about it.[2]

This is a huge dilemma—the man o' your dreams is rapidly turning day-to-day affairs, and your marriage, into Nightmare on Elm Street.

You may feel trapped. After all, he may have the larger income; who are you to complain about how it is spent?

You may feel protective. Maybe he *doesn't* provide for you and his children, but you love him so much, you believe he has what it takes. He just needs a chance.

You may feel cheated. Life could be so much more pleasant if he didn't fritter away money. You never bargained for the stress, the arguments, the lower quality lifestyle.

You may feel angry. You may feel bitterness because of his refusal to act responsibly. Rage simmers where once love filled your heart.

You may feel frightened. You feel powerless because he holds the purse strings—or spends money irresponsibly—and you know the inevitable day of reckoning awaits you.

You may have your head in the clouds. You are willing to believe in your knight in shining armor, and you continue to give him the benefit of the doubt, in spite of his obvious financial destitution.

You may feel like a hero. You will take charge, control all the money transactions, set a budget, and bail him out. Again.

What on earth do you do? Sister, pray for your man. Get on your prayer bones. If necessary, pray that your husband will become responsible with money, or responsible toward you, by not leaving you in the dark.

It may very well be up to you to *pray* for change and be a

part of change in the house, if you want your husband to budge. Your prayer might sound like this:

> *Righteous heavenly Father, you know my heart and you know my circumstance. I pray with all of my heart that you would grant grace and mercy, and direct my husband to communicate with me about money management. I pray also, Father, that you would soften my heart and heal my wounds. Help me to show my husband respect, I beseech you, in the name of your precious Son, Jesus.*

What else can you do?

1. *Get to the root of the problem.* This may mean convincing him to meet with counselors who can discuss his spending patterns, and determine if there are underlying sins or internal factors involved.
2. *Set limits.* Be prepared for some fallout when spending limits are established. If you "lay down the law," so to speak, there may be some rough sledding ahead, as he may challenge or defy any parameters.
3. *Your husband needs to become accountable.* A trusted friend, a pastor, or a financial counselor can become a very important team player right now.

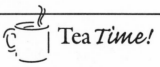 Tea *Time!*

Do I respect my husband? If not, what can I do to change my attitude?

Now that we've discussed your significant other, what about the children?

What Are You Teaching Your Kids About Money?

The Bible tells us in Proverbs 22:6 to "train a child in the way he should go, and when he is old he will not turn from it." It is incumbent upon you as a parent to teach your child thrift, as well as sound money management. How do you do that? By example.

Shortly after Josh married Molly, I overheard him say to her, "Do you want some 'walking-around' money?" I glanced over to see our son reach into his wallet and hand something to his wife as she headed out the door to go to town. Suddenly I saw my husband in that gesture.

Joseph never sat Josh down and said, "Now, when you are all grown up and married, you should ask your wife if she wants walking-around money." But Joseph asked me if I needed walking-around money a hundred times. I was shocked by the realization that children *do* watch and listen and mimic their parents. What behavior of yours will your children mimic?

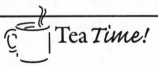 Tea *Time!*

Make the pot of tea extra hot so you can think about these questions a long time: How many times do the kids see me whip out my credit card? Do the kids hear arguments about money? Do the kids have a way of talking me into everything they want? What on earth am I teaching them?

In my book *1,001 Bright Ideas to Stretch Your Dollars,* I offer advice on keeping the kids out of the expensive cereal aisle at the market. But having children is a lot more than worrying about Sugarfrostedfluffio's. Demands on the pocketbook are relentless; from care to feeding to education to clothes, kids are an expensive proposition. There is shopping help in the last chapter; right now I want to address the specific issue of the needs, wants, and desires of that insatiable little consumer of yours. Here are my suggestions.

Mute the TV commercials. How I wish families would do away with television altogether. The message it puts in those innocent little minds is frightful, and the constant onslaught of commercials downright criminal. If you, an adult, can be seduced into buying a product because of its dramatic claims and punchy jingle, think how a child's mind is affected. This is a worrisome predicament. Just think of the phenomenally high cost of toy sets that accompany children's motion pictures!

Set limits when your kids are in the cradle. It is easy—it is natural—to want to buy every cute baby outfit and gadget that Shoptilyoudrop & Co. has to offer. But giving in to such a desire can be your, and your kids', downfall. Cool it. For one thing, children grow too fast. For another, they need sturdy, long-wearing clothes, rather than a closet full of frills. You, not the kid, are the one getting the thrill from your child looking like a model for Madison Avenue. Give your children messages right from the beginning; teach them a simple, godly life. That is abundance enough. (Leave the armloads of gifts to the grandparents.)

Talk to your children in their language as soon as they can comprehend. "We don't do that" or "No way, Jose" just won't do. Whether you know this or not, kids live in a social world, too, and they are pressured to fit in. Peer pressure is a big issue for children, especially adolescents and teens. Simply crossing your arms and slamming your foot down might create hurt and rebellion in your kids.

Define financial parameters to the children. Assemble bills and notepad (or gather the material you've written down on the charts in this book). Convene a family meeting when no one is hurried. The purpose of the meeting is to show the kids your income and outgo. Use dollar bills and coins—or beans—to illustrate.

Ask them what they think they could do, individually or corporately, to cut back or to save. Provide incentive for good behavior: a "recreation" or "vacation" jar to collect savings.

One more thing: Don't deny your kids everything. There is nothing wrong with treating your child to something wished-for, once in a while.

Should You Give an Allowance?

I think so. And there is nothing wrong with encouraging enterprise in a motivated child, either. When I was young I not only sold wildflowers to neighbors, I collected newspapers and rags to sell to the junk dealer. As soon as I was old enough, I baby-sat and got part-time jobs. Children today can collect aluminum cans for recycling, and can deliver papers, or baby-sit.

The amount of allowance should be within reason, for both

you and your child. Certainly a child living in an urban setting might need more pocket change than a child living on a farm. But there must be strings attached to an allowance.

Decide whether or not you are paying your child for chores performed at home. We did not believe Josh should be paid for doing his fair share in the family, but we did offer him a "bonus" when he did something extra.

I'd recommend a written contract that outlines exactly what items the child is fiscally responsible for. These might include such things as movies, video rentals, fast-food snacks, a school lunch; or personal items such as school supplies, clothes, savings, gifts.

Money and Thee: Finding Your Way

There is one thing I am sure we can agree on: Love and money can sometimes be troublesome partners! Take heart, my friend, and seek the Lord's grace for overcoming destructive behavior, for preparing your husband's heart, for healing your husband's habits, or for training up your children to be good stewards of God's providence. And now that we've all had a dose of guilt, maybe it's a good time to take a look at our savings strategy.

Whether it's in the middle of an argument, or teaching money management principles to children, or during evaluation of personal spending habits, emphasis is usually on one particular issue: savings. Newspaper headlines scream at us, as if we needed reminding, "Americans Not Saving!" "Very Few Americans Saving for Retirement!" Is your lack of savings causing you sleepless nights? Would you be soaked to the bone on a rainy day? Buck up, buckaroo, the next chapter is for you!

Take a minute to think about your next purchase. Ask your-self, "Do I gotta have it?"

Now it's your turn to write. Think about what you've read in this chapter. How does it apply to you? Soul-search a little, and jot down your thoughts.

Where I am now: _____

_____

_____

Where I'd like to be: _____

_____

_____

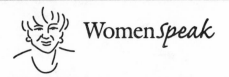 Women *Speak*

"Keep a liquid contingency fund. This is *not* your savings account. If you own a car, for instance, how smart is it to save on car insurance by keeping a high deductible when you don't even have enough saved to pay the deductible? If you own a home, your contingency fund should be enough, say, to replace a refrigerator or washing machine or lawn mower, just in case. You don't have to be a pessimist to plan for costly disasters."

———

"Invest for the long-term in low- to high-risk ventures. Don't pass up a 401(k), and put in greater than the minimum to get a company match. Even if you pull out before you're fully vested, you'll still end up with more capital than you personally put in. And don't be afraid of risk. Investment companies stake their reputations on investing other people's money wisely. I tried reading books on investing, but I don't have the time or interest to learn the world of investing."

———

"Keep a savings account, but don't keep everything in your savings account. Put your money in short-term investments, like CDs or bonds, so that you'll have enough for a decent down payment to take the sting out of the interest you'll pay on the mortgage or car loan. I've recently learned that the interest a savings account accrues doesn't even keep up with the cost of living. If you want to invest in a CD, check out credit card company offerings. I've invested in a couple of CDs that have offered rates around .5 percent above what any banks in town were offering."

seven

Saving, Saving ... Even on Bumpy Seas

When *Family Circle* spotlighted Oseola McCarty in their April 22, 1997, issue, it was because the elderly black washerwoman had donated her life savings to a scholarship fund for African-American students. We should learn from this Mississippi woman who just scratched by, and still managed to save. Here is one of her principles: "You've got to leave investment alone long enough for it to increase."[1]

A good paraphrase for Oseola's savings strategy might be, "A watched pot never boils!" or, simply, "Hands Off!"

Many of us wish we had savings to put our hands *on!* More than one woman has told me of her feeling of guilt or frustration at the very mention of savings. I doubt there are many people alive who are not aware of the importance of putting something aside for tomorrow. Saving for a special purchase or for retirement is often something we *intend* to do—sort of an "I'll save for tomorrow ... *tomorrow*" attitude. We can easily feel discouragement when we read a book like this one, and hear about a woman *who washed other people's clothes all her life* and managed to save! Some of us feel like complete zeros—a good match with our savings account. Yet we are not alone. People have difficulty saving money, for a myriad of reasons.

Our Reasons for Not Saving

People don't save money for lots of reasons ... most of which are rationalizations or excuses:

1. *"I don't need to save money ... I'm trusting God to supply all my needs!"* No question that our security rests in God alone, not in how much money we have in the bank. Money is temporal, and as we've already learned, we are stewards of money and possessions, which belong to the Lord. But as stewards, or managers, we are accountable for the way we handle what has been entrusted to us. To whom are we accountable? To God.

2. *"I'm not disciplined."* Americans are not accustomed to thinking about saving. From the boom-time of war years, and into easy credit, saving *any*thing has not been part of our national character. We are constantly asked to buy the latest, and the most improved. We neither learn to care for what we have (and make it last) nor put money away for tomorrow.

Discipline is hard, but we can develop it. Here are two ideas for how to exercise discipline to save some money. In order to prove to yourself that you can learn to live on less of each paycheck, try this: Put one penny in ten into a sock or jar, for a couple of weeks. Touching the money is *verboten*. Or, deny yourself one routine treat this week, and put that money aside for savings.

3. *"I don't have enough money to make an investment."* While you need a certain amount of money to open an investment account, you will never have a lot more money unless you start saving something. *You have to start.* Think about Oseola, the woman I mentioned earlier. It's a good thing for the students she's helping that she didn't say, "All I have is a couple of dollars; it's not worth the effort." Oseola is proof that it *is* worth the effort.

Build on what you have, no matter how small. Put some money into a savings account each month, and let it earn interest while you add to it. Once you have a "minimum" amount for investment, then invest that little bundle and start over again. Incidentally, United States Savings Bonds are particularly useful if you save in small increments, because they are available in amounts as low as $50, which are purchased at 50 percent of value.

4. *"I can't afford to save."* Very few of us ever find the right time to save money. Yet, we do what we want to do in life—including save money. It is a matter of priorities. No matter how much we make, we manage to live on that amount. Remember Oseola.

If you haven't begun to save, start now, no matter what your age. Naturally, the younger you are, the less money you must invest, and the more your money will work for you. When you are young, you can always wait for tomorrow. When you are old, tomorrow is yesterday. *That is why so many experts try to convince young people to begin saving for retirement no later than age twenty-five.*

If you are starting later in life, your money will have to work harder. It's never too late to save for the future. As usual, to do so, you need a plan.

Tea *Time!* for the Under 50 Set

Forget about today for a minute, and think about yourself at age sixty-five. Will your children be grown and married? Will you be married? Will you have grandchildren? Will you be living in the same house, town, state, country? Will you be healthy? Will you be dependent or independent? Will you be peaceful, or filled with anxiety? How long will you live beyond age 65—to 70? 75? 85? 90? Will you still eat, wear clothes, and need a roof over your head?

Here are some tips for increasing the amount of money you can save:

- Use things up. Find extra money every other week by skipping grocery shopping and using food on hand. Cook the oatmeal, defrost the burger, make pie with that can of pumpkin. Put the money saved into your savings account.
- Talk with your insurance agent about raising your deductibles on home and auto. I favor a high deductible on homeowners ($1,000) since concern here is for catastrophe. Consider higher deductibles on collision and comprehensive car coverage. If your car is financed, you may not be allowed to go too high with deductibles, so check into this. When considering raising deductibles, *evaluate the actual savings against your risk.* It is risky to maintain a high deductible if you do not have an emergency fund to cover the deductible.
- Unless you have a responsible agent who will do this for you, shop for the best insurance premium for the coverage you want. Keep in mind that switching companies can keep you from developing a favorable history with a company, and the discount that goes with that. If savings is substantial, though, and *coverage is the same or better,* you may want to switch.
- Say no to impulse buying for a week, then a month.
- If you are not using something (a set of skis, a freezer, a

sewing machine), sell it through the local trading paper.

- Call your credit card company and ask for a no-fee card and lower interest.
- If you will save at least 2 percent interest, and plan on staying there for a while to offset the new closing costs, refinance your home.
- Check with your bank to see if you can get standard transaction fees waived, or free checks.
- Become energy efficient. For instance, by turning your hot water heater down from 140 degrees to 120 degrees, you can save as much as 12 percent on hot water bills. My book *1,001 Bright Ideas To Stretch Your Dollars* offers other ideas and tips.
- Take a look at your phone bills. See if you can do better with another service company. Cut back on your long-distance calls.

Once you develop frugal habits and learn to live within your means, you will start to accumulate extra money. What better thing to do with that money than to invest it in savings?

How Should I Invest My Money?

When I was trained to sell insurance and mutual funds, I learned an important principle in financial management: Keep a balanced portfolio. In other words, don't put all your eggs in one basket. The term for this principle in financial circles is *asset allocation*, which is the process of combining different types of investments into a portfolio designed to meet an investor's needs. It is also called *diversification*.

This is good advice. When your investments are diversified,

you balance your risk, and short of national economic failure, you can usually weather a storm. Here's what I mean: If only part of your investments are in stocks, and the stock market takes a belly dive, only *part* of your investment portfolio is impacted negatively.

Mary Alice had all her eggs in one basket—real estate. She had always believed that owning rental property and land was the only sure and safe investment. "When you own land," said her dad, "you've got something." Real estate is often a good investment, but not that time. Poor Mary Alice. Her two buildings and vacant lot plummeted in value when a rendering plant was built nearby. If Mary Alice had invested only part of her money in real estate, she would not have suffered such complete loss. Incidentally, most financial planners advise caution about investing in real estate—they've seen severe financial problems many times, as a result of these investments.

Diversification applies to the risk factor of investment, as well. Consider the stock market again. As you will learn, some stocks are less risky than others, and while they may not perform dramatically, they plod along with their somewhat predictable return. So, if you are risk-diversified, you have some high-risk investments and some that are low-risk.

Let's take a look at specific places where you can invest your money.

Savings Account
Putting money in a traditional savings account is, in a word, unwise. Savings accounts pay low interest, compared to what you can get elsewhere. One advantage, however, is that your savings is insured (up to $100,000) to protect you from loss.

You should only consider putting your money into savings for two reasons:

1. As a readily accessible fund for an emergency. It makes sense to have a few months' salary tucked away.
2. As a starting-off point to get you on the road to saving. (Note: Every child should have a savings account to develop the discipline of saving.)

Emergency Fund

Most experts say you should save three to six months worth of salary, in case of emergencies such as unexpected car repairs, medical bills, travel, or home or appliance repair. This makes a lot of sense. For one thing, you want to be able to access money without penalty. If all your money is tied up in CDs, for instance, you would take a beating if you had to cash some in.

Check with banks, savings and loans, and credit unions to see where you will get the highest rate of interest. Be careful to protect your relationship with your bank, though, before you shop for interest rates; it may make sense for you to settle for one-quarter of 1 percent less in interest, as a show of good faith to your banker.

It is common for people to keep their emergency funds in an interest-bearing checking account at their bank. Note: This is not a "household" checking account, but an *emergency fund.*

Once you have the recommended amount in your emergency fund, you should then invest your money in places that will yield higher interest rates.

Money Market Accounts

Offered through banks, these funds pay higher interest than savings accounts, and they allow you to write checks (usually stipulating a minimum check amount, which may be $100 or even $250). Federal regulation allows a maximum of six withdrawals (three of which may be checks) from the account per month. Money markets are subject to minimum deposits, and can be redeemed at any time.

Certificates of Deposit
Under this arrangement, the bank (or whoever guarantees the CD) agrees to pay a higher rate of interest, based on how long you agree to leave your money in the account.

Certificates of deposit have minimum deposit requirements, some as low as $500. A certificate of deposit rewards you with higher interest because you guarantee you will leave money in the account for a specific amount of time, ranging anywhere from three months to sixty months.

CDs cannot be cashed without penalty before they mature, so be sure that the money you invest in a CD is money you don't plan on needing during the allotted amount of time. Banks and other lending companies sometimes offer their own CDs, and will often custom-tailor one for you. There is such a thing as a CD loan, however, which is one step up from a passbook loan. It lets you use your funds prior to maturity at a nominal cost, and makes a good first credit experience.

Stocks
For many, the world of stocks and bonds is mysterious and scary. What follows is some basic information to help you better understand how to navigate this world.

What is the stock market? To explain, I'm going to talk about the grocery market. We buy all kinds of groceries: dairy, grains and cereals, meat and fish, fruit and veggies, canned goods. To buy these different groceries, we go to a grocery market. There are several different markets in town: some with big names that are part of a national chain, some that are local markets. What's more, we have warehouse markets, outlets, and farmer's markets.

Sometimes we just go "grocery shopping," and sometimes we shop with a list. Sometimes our list is general—the fridge is empty. Sometimes our list is specific—"chocolate-covered aardvark lips."

Such is the *stock market,* an array of markets for such things as stocks and bonds. Some of the markets' names are the New York Stock Exchange, the American Stock Exchange, the National Association of Securities Dealers Automated Quotation System (NASDAQ), the over-the-counter market, not to mention regional and local exchanges in key cities.

What is stock? A stock is a certificate of ownership of a company. The company offers stock for sale to accumulate capital for operations, expansion, and so on. If, for instance, Shoptilyoudrop & Co. decided to sell stock, and you bought one share, you would own a portion of Shoptilyoudrop & Co.

Furthermore, there are *common stocks* and *preferred stocks.* If you own common stock, your dividend is based on the performance of the company. If the company has done a bang-up job selling its product, you get a bigger dividend. If you own preferred stock, you get your dividend checks before common stockholders get theirs, and if Shoptilyoudrop & Co. goes belly-up, any money left over after creditors goes first to the preferred holders, then to the common stock holders.

Should you "play" the market? If by that, you mean, should you buy a computer program, and spend eight hours every day evaluating the complex world of finance, and invest your money by yourself, I don't think so. You should, however, spend some *effort and time* to evaluate your investment, stay informed, and seek counsel. Consult a broker or financial planner with experience and savvy. Short of the world coming to an end, you will probably do OK in the market if you don't wince every time it takes a dive. And besides, your money is in other places as well. Right?

What are growth and income stocks? Today's financial world offers complex and sophisticated opportunities for finding a balance between risk and reward—growth and income. A growth stock can be high risk. Many times these stocks are offered by a cutting-edge company, though they can sometimes be offered by solid blue chip companies. If you invest in a growth stock, you stand to win—or lose—big.

Income stocks, on the other hand, are the old faithful "meat and potatoes" of the stock market. They are generally low-risk, and consistently produce a productive return. A good example of an income stock would be utilities.

Mutual Funds

A popular investment option, mutual funds are usually made up of combinations of different stocks and/or bonds. A mutual fund takes seriously the adage "Don't put all your eggs in one basket." Though you invest your money in a particular fund, say the "Shopping Fund," the administrators of that fund assess the marketplace and invest in a cluster of different businesses. For instance, the administrators of the "Shopping Fund" might decide to buy a whole block of shares in the up-and-coming Shoptilyoudrop & Co., because they have buying power with the money from people like you who invest in their fund. Shoptilyoudrop will only be one of several companies the Shopping Fund invests in. A fund might invest only in government bonds, foreign stocks, real estate, or a mix. Find a mutual fund that has sound management and good investment savvy. By checking with reporting agencies (Morningstar, S & P), you will be able to look at the track record and rating of a fund. The best bet, in my opinion, is to check with a reputable source—a professional, such as a stockbroker or certified financial planner.

When you buy shares in a mutual fund, you are not buying the individual stocks in which they've invested, but shares in the fund itself. A share represents the net asset value of all the stocks and bonds in a mutual fund portfolio, divided by the number of shares outstanding. (You theoretically own a little bit of everything.) The fund will distribute dividends to the shareholders based on performance.

In the world of mutual funds, there are "closed-end" funds (bought on the Exchange) and "open-end" funds (bought through an investment company.) The closed-end fund just makes a certain number of shares available, and that's it. The open fund will continually offer its shares to the public.

Some people believe that if they purchase mutual funds on their own, they will bypass the commission. This is sort of true. Somebody, whether a stockbroker or the company itself, will normally get a commission. You can buy funds over the phone from companies that deal directly with the public; you can buy funds through your job if they offer such options through payroll deduction; or you can buy through a licensed financial planner or broker. It is true that if you go through a broker, you will pay an additional charge.

If a fund is called a "load" fund, that means there is a sales charge. At this writing, a typical sales charge is around 5.75

percent. If a fund is "no load," that means it does not have a sales charge.

There are creative variations to the load fund, such as back load and front load. Depending on your agreement, you would pay a sales fee if you left the fund early (back load) or you pay the fee right up front (front load). The offer price contains the front load. If you are buying back load, you pay no fee at all, but buy "net asset value." Only if you liquidate the fund (usually within six years) is there a fee, and it is a declining fee. There is also something called low load. This means you are usually charged 1 percent going in, and 1 percent a year. This fee adds up, but if you want something for the short term, this is a nice option.

All funds—load or no-load—have management fees. No-loads may have higher advertising/marketing fees, since they don't have a sales force. A typical management fee is around .5 percent of the net assets. Your account is debited for management fees each year.

Money Market Funds

A money market fund is essentially a mutual fund that has a limit of $1 per share. Money markets are short-term investments, and do not pay a high yield. Their interest rates vary daily. You can usually do better here than with a regular bank savings account. Since it is a mutual fund, there is risk involved, but the risk could be considered quite a bit less than the regular market, since it invests in short-term securities, such as treasury bills.

The only significant differences between the money market account at a bank and a money market mutual fund are:

- The bank's account is insured up to $100,000 by the federal government; there is no insurance on the fund account.
- Interest rates are pretty much equal with each other, the fund *sometimes* having an edge on the bank. Both accounts are usually considered a place where you can "park your money" short-term, or they make great emergency fund savings accounts, because your money remains accessible and earns some interest at the same time.

Bonds and Notes

When you buy a bond, you are not *investing* in a company, but *loaning* money to a company (or municipality) for a certain period of time, with guarantee of repayment with interest. What's more, the company "selling" the bond backs up its promise to repay with assets that could include real estate, buildings, even office furniture. So, if the company goes belly-up, and there is foreclosure, you, as a bondholder, are entitled to some kind of reparation. Not only that, as a bondholder you would be first in line to collect, after bankruptcy court liquidated assets. Worth noting is the relationship between bond prices and interest rates. It is said that when interest rates rise, bond prices fall; when interest rates fall, bond prices often rise.

Where do you buy bonds? Brokers usually charge a minimum fee for a bond trade, still it may be advantageous to hold the bond in your brokerage account for security or liquidity. If you pay a commission to a securities dealer or broker, you may be offsetting the interest you'd make. If you are buying U.S. government bonds, you might want to turn to a Federal Reserve bank. If you buy from the Federal Reserve, be sure to inform them that you are a private investor, and are not interested in competitive bidding. (The price to you will end up being the average of all the competitive bids.) Watch newspapers such as the *Wall Street Journal* for announcements of bond sales.

There are several types of bonds:

Treasuries. These are offered by the U.S. government, and while not entirely risk-free, are probably the safest investment. Treasuries can be purchased through a broker, or through a Federal Reserve bank. They include:

- Treasury bond (T-bond). These offer a fixed rate and require a minimum investment. Treasury bonds are exempt from state and local taxes. Interest is paid semi-annually. Money is invested for over ten years.

- Treasury note (T-note).These offer a fixed rate and require a minimum investment. Interest is paid semi-annually. Money is invested for one to ten years.

- Treasury bill (T-bill). This is a bit like a government version of a short-term certificate of deposit, and require a minimum investment. When you purchase a T-Bill, you pay less than the face value, the difference between what you paid and the face value being your "interest." These are short-term investments, up to one year.

- Savings (EE) bond. This bond is purchased at a bank or credit union for half the face value. These bonds are available in $50, $75, $100, $1,000, $5,000, and $10,000 denominations. An EE Bond will accrue interest for up to thirty years. Logically, the longer a bond is held, the greater the payoff to the investor. EE bonds can be redeemed as soon as six months from purchase, though they do not reach their maturity (face value) for eighteen years. Bond rates follow market rates.

Federal agencies. Some federal agencies issue bonds, which can be purchased through a bank or stockbroker. Federal agency bonds are called Ginnie Mae (Government National Mortgage Association), Sallie Mae (Student Loan Corporation), Fannie Mae (Federal Home Loan Bank), and Freddie Mac (Federal Home Loan Mortgage Company). Though these bond issues often require participation in the tens of thousands of dollars, they are usually considered safe, and offer a good return, though certain types of mortgage-backed securities can be considered risky. When you buy into a federal agency bond, you are buying into a "pool." The interest rate changes daily; anyone with a sizable amount of money to invest can get them; and they can be purchased through a broker. For the person with a little capital and some investment savvy, federal agency bonds offer a little challenge (and I'm told, fun!) to an investment portfolio.

Municipal bonds. Municipal bonds are "floated" when a municipality wants cash to accomplish something, like build a school or a bridge. Municipal bonds are exempt from federal tax and can be exempt from state and local taxes. Some people invest in municipal bonds for personal reasons. For instance, they may purchase a bond through the school district to help raise money for a new computer lab in the high school. The municipal bond rate is, literally, what the market will bear. The ideal is to offer a rate that will attract investors. An average term is from five to fifteen years.

Zero-coupon bonds (usually government issues). Similar to a T-bill, the zero-coupon bond is bought for a reduced price, perhaps half of the maturity payoff. It does not offer any interest during the term of the bond. You simply cash it in at maturity and collect your payment. A zero-coupon bond would make a lot of sense for the younger crowd, because it is a great method to save money without investing much up front.

Not all bonds come from the federal government or from government agencies.

Corporate bonds. These are private bonds offered from the world of business. Bonds allow a business to take a "loan" from investors, who now become bondholders. Corporate bonds carry varying degrees of risk. People typically pay $1,000 a bond, and lock into a certain number of years.

When considering any bond, check its rating. Turn to Moody's or the S & P Bond Rating Schedules. These resources can be found at your public library, or you can count on your broker to inform you. These rating agencies just look at the credit quality of a company.

- AAA means very, very low risk
- AA means very low risk
- A means low risk
- B means some risk
- C means better be careful

This, by no means, has been an exhaustive review of the world of investments, just an overview to acquaint you with some terms. If you want to try your hand at investing, and want to dig a bit deeper, there is one book I heartily recommend, *Put Your Money Where Your Heart Is* by Sherman Smith, Ph.D.

Should You Invest On Your Own?

Unless you have time to keep abreast of all the tax laws *(and no financial advisor should ever invest without considering the tax advantages or disadvantages for the client);* market swings; economic indicators; best buys, worst buys; short-term bonanzas; long-term payoffs; high risk, low risk; diversification; and so on, get a financial counselor when you are ready to make a serious investment. Financial advisors and brokers are subject to tough regulations, and face severe consequence if they violate rules. As Sherman Smith says about finding a top-drawer financial advisor: "This is perhaps among the most important decisions you can make as you seek to maximize your financial health. Much more important than, say, deciding that now is the time to buy IBM stock. Finding the right professional to act as your advisor is critical."[2]

Should you depend on your insurance agent, your accountant, or your banker for this advice? Many advisers say no. *Not unless he or she is highly qualified in all areas of investment.* Look for an investment professional who can, for a fee, provide everything you need, such as tax advice, a formal financial plan for your goals, insurance, stocks, bonds, and management of your investment portfolio. A typical fee might run from $75 to $100 per hour. There may be a flat fee of $500 to $1,000, though, depending upon the complexity of the plan.

Of course, you can do most everything yourself. You can purchase books and software that will guide you through the investment maze. But will the computer program look you in the eye and ask personal questions to determine the best approach for you? Probably not. A good working relationship with a certified financial planner might be worth its weight in dividends.

A Word About Investment Clubs

Clarice was flabbergasted when she got the news: She and her brother had just inherited $2 million. It seems her father had parlayed his small weekly paycheck into a serious stock portfolio over the years, and upon his death his two children were suddenly in the chips. "I never had money before," said Clarice, "but I wanted to follow in Dad's footsteps, and see what I could do in the market." Armed with a library book on establishing an investment club, and a lot of determination, Clarice started an investment club in her town. She was part of a new breed of investors—savvy people around the country (including many, many women) who pool their money and knowledge in order to play the stock and fund market.

An investment club may be for you. It is a group of between ten and twenty people (any more makes it untenable), who meet at least once each month. Each member contributes a predetermined amount of money, say $50, though there are clubs that get along nicely on $20 monthly payments from each member. An investment club can be a source of great satisfaction, and personal and financial growth. If poorly managed or poorly attended, however, it can also be a source of great disappointment.

In her book *Investment Clubs: A Low Cost Education in the Stock Market,* Kathryn Shaw encourages a mix of members who will share the same sense of responsibility. Keep in mind there will be legal requirements, including tax consequence. Shaw suggests certain criteria for establishing a club, which I have expanded upon:

- commitment

- developing an investment philosophy
- determining regularity of investing
- proper market timing
- reinvestment strategies
- a mission statement (a woman after my own heart)
- a name for your club...how about "The Proverbs 31 Women"? [3]

For specific information on investment clubs, contact the National Association of Investors Corporation (NAIC) for its book *Starting and Running a Profitable Investment Club.* Or access its Web site: http://www.better-investing.org.

Tea *Time!*

Since you can buy shares in a mutual fund for as little as $25, saving enough to buy into a mutual fund is a short-term goal with an eye toward long-term investment. Saving for a car or vacation is a short-term goal. Saving for retirement or your child's college education is long term. What are your short-term financial goals? What are your long-term financial goals?

Money and Thee: Finding Your Way

We've certainly come a long way from the sock with the spare change in it, buried in the backyard! As you've seen, there are many options (and options within options) available to everyone who has money to invest. Investing and saving can be fun, as you work toward short-term and long-term goals, and see your wise choices and the sacrifice of your efforts pay off. One huge goal we all face, some of us sooner than later, is retirement. How prepared are you for your twilight years?

Now it's your turn to write. Think about what you have read in this chapter. How does it apply to you? Soul-search a little, and jot down your thoughts.

Where I am now: _____

_____

_____

Where I'd like to be: _____

_____

_____

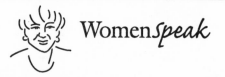 Women *Speak*

"The smartest thing a woman can do to protect herself financially is to start saving for retirement. You can't start too soon, and it's only going to get more expensive to maintain your lifestyle. (Maybe a footnote should be: Educate your children and make sure they have fabulous incomes, because we want them to take care of us in our old age ...)"

———

"The biggest mistake I ever made when it comes to money: I wish I had started allotting monies, however small, to savings and investments, from my earliest earning days."

———

"Tell other women to learn from me. Look at me. I could have saved, but I didn't. Now it's too late. I'm stuck in low-income housing and have to depend on my kids to pay for any extras."

eight

A Gold Watch, a Handshake, and a Pension ... Maybe

At fifty, I am eyeing retirement. And so will you, if you aren't already. What will you be eyeing in the future? A little nest egg, which is growing, and will provide you comfort and security? Or are you among the high percentage of people who will retire at a lower standard of living?

Experts say that people simply don't plan properly for their retirement needs. You may be "planning without a plan"—planning to work till the day you die; planning to stay perfectly healthy and strong, so you *can* work to the day you die; planning for your husband to stay perfectly healthy, and work until the day *he* dies; or planning to continue to live comfortably, even if your husband dies. You may also be "planning" to be dependent on grown children, to live in near-poverty conditions, to face years of anxiety and anguish over paying bills. *Some plan, huh.*

To realistically make a plan for retirement, you must know how much you need to save in order to retire on the income you will need at that time. An article in *Christian American* gives this simple rule of thumb: For every $1,000 needed in monthly income, you will need a savings of $250,000, earning 5 percent; you will need $150,000 in savings if the money is earning at least 8 percent. [1]

Ouch.

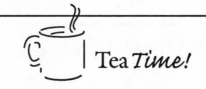
Tea *Time!*

Have you ever thought about how much money you will need to live on in order to retire? Scratch out where you expect to be at the age you hope to retire: Will the mortgage be paid by then? Will all of your children be out of the home and on their own? Will costly loans be long paid? How much does it cost you to live now? Subtract the monthly costs that will be "retired" right along with you, then add upward to 25 percent to compensate for inflation and new costs (higher insurance premiums, medical bills). Once you determine your projected monthly costs, try to extend that cost into years you "expect" to live—I'm shooting for 120, how about you?! This process is easily tackled, with the help of a highly trained insurance professional or financial planner.

Once you determine how much income you will need to retire comfortably, you must consider your sources for that income.

Sources of Retirement Income

Social Security

Some claim that Social Security is going the way of the dinosaur; some say it is here to stay (in one fashion or another). Regardless, Social Security doesn't promise you a tea party. It should be considered as only part of your retirement income. To estimate your retirement income from Social

Security, call their 800 number, and ask for a projection of your income.

Employee Retirement Plans

If you are in a vested plan at work, you can ask for a projection of estimated retirement income. Find out what kind of plan your employer participates in, how reliable it is, what the history of the plan is, how it is backed, and if you have other options. This is your money, after all.

Qualified pension plans have lost a little limelight through the years, because of a corporation's minimum funding requirement and the harsh financial consequences if the plan is underfunded. Many corporations are turning to deferred profit-sharing (401(k)) plans for employee retirement benefits. Under a deferred profit-sharing plan, a specified percentage (with no guarantees of specific amounts) of company profits is invested into a qualified profit-sharing plan. This is different from a qualified pension plan, which is subject to investment amounts called for by the plan itself.

Deferred profit-sharing plans are dependent upon company profits.

Individual Retirement Accounts (IRAs)

A common retirement plan for working and nonworking women is the Individual Retirement Account, or IRA. This allows people to invest up to a certain amount each year, and deduct it from their tax return. (At this writing, the maximum contribution is $2,000.) You can invest through a bank, through some mutual funds, or even through other intangible investments, such as stocks. Banks often compete for IRA funds, and may offer appealing guaranteed interest rates.

Mutual funds, on the other hand, offer greater payoff, but some risk as well.

The immediate benefit of an IRA account is the investing of your pretax dollar. For instance, if you were in a 15 percent tax bracket and earned $100.00, your taxes would be $15.00. If you deducted $10.00 for your IRA pretax, you would only be taxed on $90.00 and pay $13.50 in tax. You pay penalty *and* tax if you withdraw IRA funds before age fifty-nine-and-a-half, and will pay tax on any withdrawals after that time. If you let your money sit in the IRA account after you are seventy-and-a-half, the IRS will begin to penalize you. And it's nasty. The government intends to get its taxes somehow. If you do not begin to withdraw from your IRA by December 30 of the year you turn seventy-and-a-half, as much as 50 percent of the amount of your minimum distribution will be demanded as tax. Changes in the tax code, and rules governing IRAs, and such, are changing regularly. Check with a professional to stay up-to-date.

Some financial consultants refer to any tax-deferred investments as a tax time bomb. They have a point. Many of us have invested in pensions and IRAs, expecting that two things will be to our benefit when we retire: (1) We will be in a much lower tax bracket, due to reduced income, and therefore the tax penalty on withdrawing from our tax-deferred funds will be lessened. (2) Government regulations on taxes will not change to our detriment by the time we retire.

Some experts believe it is best to do what you can to minimize tax penalty now, rather than face uncertain tax laws in the future. Their position is in contrast to conventional wisdom, which encourages you to invest pretax dollars now, and "take your lumps" later. You should take a common-sense approach to all of your investments and consider both sides of the coin. As one financial writer put it, nothing should be done with your assets, whether by you or your representative (investment counselor, stockbroker) without first considering tax consequence.[2]

Roth IRAs

There is a new player on the field: an IRA that is funded with after-tax dollars, thereby allowing you tax-free withdrawals. The principal accrues tax-free. It is called a Roth IRA. A Roth IRA should be considered on an individual basis. Some people convert their traditional IRA to a Roth, even though they have to pay taxes on the converted amount. Stop by your bank and grab an explanatory brochure on the merits of a Roth. For some, this is a very attractive deal. This investment opportunity seems like a compromise between those who counsel you to take those lumps now, and those who promote tax-deferred investments.

Simplified Employee Pension (SEP IRAs) & Keogh

If you are self-employed, you may invest up to 15 percent or $30,000 of your self-employed income into a SEP-IRA. (If you have employees, you may have to make a like contribution at the same rate.) If you retrieve your funds before age fifty-nine-and-a-half, you will be subject to penalty, unless you begin a lifetime distribution program. You will be penalized if you don't begin to withdraw funds by age seventy-and-a-half.

Named after the man who designed the program, the old trusty standby for the self-employed, however, remains the Keogh. (A Keogh requires that you make similar investments for employees, but it is more flexible than a SEP, since it requires participation only if employees have been with you for a certain period of time, or from the start of your business.) Under a Keogh you may contribute 25 percent of your net income, or a maximum of $30,000. Distribution of money (not borrowed funds) from the Keogh before age fifty results in a penalty, and you must begin to withdraw funds by age seventy-and-a-half.

Both Keoghs and SEPs are good programs for the self-employed (you cannot be incorporated). Like some other programs, you invest your money, and the government gives you tax relief. In order to have either plan, you must have a source of self-employed income, and your income must be profitable. (You can only invest based on *net* earnings.) This is one aspect that makes these programs different from a corporate plan. A corporation can base contributions on income, while SEP and Keogh contributions must be based on net income. It gets a little complicated here, so if you're interested, talk with a specialist.

401(k)

This plan is defined by the employer, and provides for pretax investment by the employee. The employer contributes to the employee's plan and often matches the employee's contribution. Some employers may even allow the employee to direct unused sick pay or vacation pay into their plans. The money in a 401(k) can be invested in a diversity of places, and run the gamut from conservative to risky investments. With a 401(k) you have a higher ceiling for pretax dollars than in an IRA. Many financial experts counsel clients to invest in an IRA each year, as well as a 401(k). If husband and wife each participate in a 401(k), it is wise to manage the plans together, and to give priority to the plan with the greater employer contributions.

403(b)

A 403(b) plan is for a nonprofit group, and is less likely than a 401(k) to have employer matching funds. But many times this plan has more investment choices.

Annuities

An annuity is something you invest in to guarantee a certain income for yourself (or loved one) for a certain time. Here's how it works: Suppose you just turned fifty, and you've scratched some figures on a pad to come up with how much you will need at retirement. You could then invest in an annuity by paying a lump sum, or paying a lump sum followed by additional payments, into the annuity.

When you retire, the annuity will begin to pay. Annuities can be custom-made to pay in a lump sum, in monthly allotments, lifetime allotments, or payments to a beneficiary, if you die. The annuity grows tax-deferred. Again, the idea is that when you retire you will be in a lower tax bracket, and will pay less tax on the income from the annuity. In that regard, annuities are touted as a method to defer taxes. Remember that this assumption may prove false. Furthermore, when you purchase an annuity, your money is not available before maturity without paying a penalty.

There is such a thing as a "variable" annuity, which invests part of your investment into mutual funds. This method offers greater growth, but more risk.

Life Insurance

As someone who was once a vigorous supporter of life insurance *as an investment*, I must recant ... a little. I still believe everyone should have some amount of permanent insurance, preferably purchased at such a young age that the premiums are negligible. (A whole life policy for $100,000, purchased at age eighteen, for instance, costs around $15 per month.) One reason I emphasize this is to protect the insurability of the person. I do, however, vigorously support the need to buy term insurance, which can be viewed as supplemental insurance you "rent" when your need for high amounts of insurance is great, generally for your vulnerable years, when you have family or business responsibility. Unlike permanent insurance, which accrues a cash value, term insurance, which is significantly less expensive, merely provides a death benefit.

Money and Thee: Finding Your Way

Shouldn't we just trust God with our future? Does the Bible say anything about retirement planning? It sure does. Look again at the Proverbs 31 woman. She manages her household and her finances so well, she can laugh at the days to come.

Retirement is coming. Anyone who is in mid-life or older can look you in the eye and say, "It was just yesterday that my children were babies ... we were starting a business ... I was in college." With a little planning you can be prepared for the days to come, and laugh a little yourself.

Some of you may very well end up laughing alone—because you are suddenly on your own. Right now may be a good time to talk about two subjects no woman wants to face: widowhood or divorce.

Tea *Time!*

1. I'm prepared, so I can laugh at the days to come.
   ☐ yes ☐ no
2. I don't care about the future. ☐ yes ☐ no
3. I will never, ever get sick. ☐ yes ☐ no
4. My husband will always be there for me. ☐ yes ☐ no
5. My children will always be there for me. ☐ yes ☐ no
6. My dog will always be there for me. ☐ yes ☐ no
7. Saving money for any reason is impossible for me.
   ☐ yes ☐ no
8. I'd rather spend money on things I want now.
   ☐ yes ☐ no
9. Jesus is coming, so I don't have to worry about retirement. ☐ yes ☐ no
10. I think saving something for the future is a good idea.
    ☐ yes ☐ no

Now it's your turn to write. Think about what you have read in this chapter. How does it apply to you? Soul-search a little, and jot down your thoughts.

Where I am now: _____

_____

_____

Where I'd like to be: _____

_____

_____

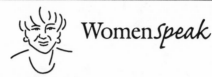

Women *Speak*

"I was so lost. It seemed as if everywhere I turned, life was rushing at me, demanding answers, decisions. This has to be done; this has to be filed; you have to pick out the casket. I was numb. All I wanted was for Tom to walk in the door like he did every night. I even hated him for dying on me. I hated everything."

———

"What people don't understand is how alone you feel. You know you have to be strong, because you have no choice, but you are miserably alone. All the financial decisions! My husband took care of everything. I had to suddenly turn into a detective and figure everything out, alone. What I didn't like was having to pick up where he left off. It brought me too close to him every time I opened another file. I should have waited longer until I began to sort through his desk, but the accountant was persistent. I feel like I was robbed of grieving for several months, until all that horrible bookwork was done."

———

"He didn't leave an updated will. His daughters from his first marriage took me to the cleaners. I'm embarrassed to say this, but the fight over his property—some of it my property—was more painful than his death. I should have been well off. Now I have to work to make ends meet, and to pay the legal fees. And it's still not over."

———

"I just wanted to die with him. And in the middle of my grief I had to deal with those stupid bills. I was a zombie."

 Women*Speak*

"What have I learned about money in eighty-one years? Invest wisely in husbands!"

———

"I know I'm supposed to say I'm sorry we are divorced, especially since I'm a Christian, but I am not sorry. I'm glad. I'm also mad. It's wrong that single moms have to kill themselves to survive, while he gets off practically scot-free. Child support from him is a joke. I know I should report him, but he will figure a way out. Besides, he's long gone, in another state. The kids haven't seen him in seven months."

———

"I tried to be fair, even to his benefit. I mean, I rolled the pennies and gave him half! And what do I get in return? A subpoena, telling me there's a lien against me because he hasn't been paying the bills he's supposed to!"

———

"I always thought we would get back together again. I dreamed about it. I tried to show him that things were different, when he came to see the kids. I even lost weight. When I heard he was getting married to someone else, my world fell apart ... for real. That's when I really got into trouble with money. Spending just made my pain go away for a while."

———

"He hit me one time too many. He thought nothing of buying toys for himself. He liked to show me off. I was one of his things. Now he wants back. It's been so hard juggling money to get along. I'm not sure what I'm going to do."

nine

On Your Own: Engaged, Widowed, or Divorced

Unless she is a nun living a cloistered life, there can only be two categories that a woman fits into: married or single. Sadly, there are two other categories that can apply to married women: widowed or divorced. Since specific financial circumstances come hand-in-hand with the loss of a husband, we need to address those issues now.

Before we get specific about widowhood or divorce, though, it makes sense to talk briefly to those women who are engaged to be married.

While You Are Still on Your Own

If you are engaged to be married, you and your fella need to be responsible in money matters—starting now. *You must include finances in your premarital counseling.* This is a biggie. At the altar, when the two of you become one, you'd better know ahead of time what the two of you are planning!

Some night, when you are gazing starry-eyed into his face, say something like:

"So, man o' my dreams, do you think retail competition in the electric market is imminent?" Once you have his attention, explain how critical it is that the two of you talk now about money.

Buy two notebooks. Write the following on the inside front cover of each: *Please answer these questions, with our marriage in mind.*

- How do you *feel* about money?
- What financial goals do you want to accomplish?
- How will you accomplish those goals?
- What are your weaknesses in money management?
- What are your strengths in money management?
- How can we help each other to guard against both of our weaknesses?

Give him a kiss on the cheek and send him home with his notebook. Remind him it is a *note* book, not a memo pad, and that this is serious business. A one-sentence answer will not do. The both of you are flushing out how you think and feel about money. Make a date, bring your homework, pray first, then share your answers.

If, during your discussions, something tugs at you—from what either one of you has said—believe me, it's a red flag. Take the tug in your spirit seriously. Seek counseling. Do *something*. Do not convince yourself "everything will work out." Work it out *now*.

Not all marriages begin with two starry-eyed young adults who are just setting out on the road to prosperity. Some people have considerable assets when they marry, and designating those assets to rightful heirs can be a serious concern. Most people do not understand the legal rights and obligations which are created when they marry. The law protects *both* spouses, and if through death or divorce your marriage should end, the law will control how your property will be divided. If you do not make advance plans, a judge will divide your assets according to the laws of your state. That is why it is so important—no matter what your age—to discuss finances *before* you marry, including your wishes for distribution of property upon your death.

When Death Leaves You on Your Own

I have never walked in your shoes, so I do not know how you feel. Even the thought of life without my Joe is more than I can bear. I am so, so sorry for you, because I suspect that in spite of rock-solid faith in the Resurrection, and of reunion in eternity, you feel alone. You may find yourself numb to emotion, or you may hurt all over. In spite of numbness or wrenching pain, dear sister, it is time to begin reconstruction of your life, with a few cautious steps.

This book is about financial management, and I will get to that in a minute. First, I want to gently encourage you to express your sorrow. Do *not* think you are unspiritual if you show your sorrow. Grieving, like healing, takes time, and depends upon a person's health, strength, and individual capacity to recover. Whether the process is fast or slow does not matter one whit. What does matter is that you honestly acknowledge your grief and allow it to flow naturally, rather than dam it up.

In the meantime, reality beckons. Widows, especially widows without adult children, have always been vulnerable in society. The Bible is a clear advocate to widows, classing them with orphans, and instructs others to provide care. In Exodus 22:22, God promises speedy revenge upon anyone who afflicts a widow.

A primary ministry of the early church was to assist widows. James wrote that true religion involved care for widows (James 1:27). We must tend to the needs of the elderly and of widows, in the tradition of the Bible. Whether you want to be there or not, you are behind the wheel. Perhaps now more than ever you must draw upon skills to manage money and to support yourself. Take a deep breath. Don't let the task ahead scare you.

Chances are, you've just been through a long bout with your husband's illness, or your husband died suddenly. In either case, you are worn out or deep in shock. This is a poor time to make life-changing decisions. Yes, some things must be done in a timely manner, but allow *yourself* some time first to adjust, and let the Holy Spirit nurture you.

Hire Professional Help

Even though you may have heard horror stories about "my accountant, my lawyer, the bank," I encourage you to enlist the aid of professionals right now. Pray over this, and look for seasoned, knowledgeable professionals who deal with estates and probate. You may need the help of an accountant, a lawyer, a banker, an insurance agent, appraisers, and an investment counselor. If it is a small estate, and there are no clouds or complications hanging over it, the family lawyer may be just fine for this task. If you are dealing with an estate of appreciable size, or if there is the slightest possibility of complication (claims by heirs, and so on), this is a time to get expert help. Track down people who specialize in this area. Consultations are usually free.

If you have trouble finding a lawyer, rely upon referrals from church members, friends, family, and associates. This may sound intimidating, but *attorneys should be interviewed no differently from any other job applicant.* Consult with more than one attorney so you can determine who will work best for you. Ask the attorney to provide you with names of others for whom they have performed a probate. Then call those people to see if there were any disputes or difficulties.

Be as prepared as possible before your meeting with any professional. Bring as much data as you can about finances. Ask whether you will be charged a flat fee, a percentage, or an hourly rate. Ask if you will be charged for phone calls, photocopies, filing fees, travel, research. Ask. Ask. Ask. And write everything down. *Caution!* This is *not* the time to clean house. If you accidentally throw away important records, you could affect the outcome of the estate settlement.

Gather the Information You Need
Sit down with every single important paper you can find. If your husband had drawers and files filled with papers, methodically go through one drawer each day. Put headings on paper: investment, insurance (life and health), associations and organizations, bank accounts, legal papers, bills, real estate, military, other. You need to know the following types of information:

Investments. Did you find dividend or account statements? Is there any kind of paperwork to indicate that your husband held stock in a company? Mutual funds? A money market account? Certificates of deposit? Read through his old checks. Did he pay a brokerage? An insurance company? Did he have a financial planner or stockbroker? Gather everything you can find, and write it on your list. Once your list is complete, find out as much as you can about each investment. Is the certificate for stocks completely worthless because it was given him by his great-grandma twice removed, and the company is long out of business? Does he have a municipal bond that will mature in three years? Who is his consultant? What must you do to change title to yourself, or to another person? Are there penalties if you cash-in now? In six months? In six years?

Insurance. Probably your husband had *some* kind of insurance. Call his agent. Also check with his parents, if possible. Some parents bought insurance on children, long ago, that might still be in effect. Check with every single organization (even credit card companies!) to see whether he has a death benefit, particularly if he died accidentally. Many fraternal organizations include a small death benefit as one of the perks of membership. Some policies have provisions that pay extra in the event of accidental death. And don't forget Social Security! There is a small (and I mean, small) death benefit payable.

Check all health insurance policies thoroughly. Some have death benefits. Also, if your husband had a lengthy illness, and coverage was denied or limited, try to submit the claim again. Be sure to deduct medical payments on your income tax. When you gather all the policies, check to see if you are the beneficiary, and if there are any distribution terms attached.

Note: There is such a thing as the National Consumer's Insurance Helpline, which operates a missing policy service. Call 1-800-555-1212 for their current 800 number, and ask for a missing policy questionnaire.

Associations and organizations. You may be entitled to death benefits. Also, determine if you want to continue membership. What are the benefits to you? It may be that the only benefit left is social encounter—a very good thing, indeed, once the hurt of his death lessens.

Bank accounts. Collect all data pertaining to his accounts. Ask for final statements from banks, if the account was in his name only. If there is an automatic deduction from his account each month (for example, homeowner's insurance), be certain there is no interruption in premium. If you and your husband had a joint safe deposit box, turn to a lawyer for advice. In some states, safe deposit boxes are sealed when someone dies.

Legal papers. Did your husband leave a will, or a trust? Gather what papers you can. Ownership papers for cars, boats, as well as deeds for real estate should be gathered. If jointly owned, it may be a simple matter of changing to the name of the sole survivor. These papers should be clipped together for your trip to the lawyer.

Bills. Your husband probably left some sort of liability, if only bills from final arrangements or from a hospital stay. There may also be a mortgage involved, child support or alimony due to a previous marriage, or outstanding loans or credit balances. Once you put everything on your list, check to see if any loans were backed by life insurance, and became fully paid upon his death.

Pensions. Does your husband have a pension plan, either privately funded through his employment (don't forget past employment!), or through the military? Make some phone calls. Check around. Find out what Social Security will pay. If there are minor children involved, be sure to consider their interests, as well.

Note: If a company your husband once worked for is now out of business, write to the Pension Benefit Guaranty Corporation, Missing Participant Program, 1200 K Street NW, Washington, DC 20005. This agency may help you locate a plan that is terminated. Include as much information as possible to help them in their search—name, address, Social Security number, date of birth, name and address of employer, as well as any documents from the plan that you might have.

Who Does What in Filing a Final Estate Tax Return?

Accountant

When it comes to filing the final estate tax return, an accountant is the captain of your team. The accountant will file Form 706, the federal tax form. This form must be completed and filed within nine months from the date of death, if an estate is valued over $600,000. In order to file the return, your husband's estate must be totally valued, and all assets and liabilities listed. This may or may not be a simple matter.

The complexity of probate is determined to a greater degree by what the deceased left behind, not if there was or was not a will. In informal probate, little needs to be appraised. Even real estate only needs to be "informally" appraised, such as by a real estate broker. However, in situations where a Form 706 is required, formal appraisal may be a good idea, to make it more bullet-proof. Formal appraisal is also recommended where there may be disputes among heirs as to the value of property.

Any form of income or expense from the estate has to be considered, right up to the moment Form 706 is filed. Income tax complications, business evaluation, state or local taxes—all must be turned into neat columns of numbers on tax returns. You most definitely need the help of someone experienced!

Lawyer

If an accountant is the team captain, your lawyer is the umpire. It is up to a practiced lawyer to guide you through the maze of estate settlement, or probate. Again, this will be as easy or as hard as whatever plan you have in effect at the time of your husband's death. If there was no will, the attorney has to follow rules of probate and deal with the court. If there was a will or a trust in place, the attorney needs to guide you (and the other professionals) through the right doorways to transfer assets with as little loss or aggravation as possible.

Banker
Unless named as executor or trustee, the banker will provide a final statement of all bank accounts at the time of death.

Life Insurance Agent
Needless to say, an agent will help you with the death claim, to obtain life insurance benefits. Your agent may also alert you to settlement options. If an annuity was in place, an accounting will also be provided.

Investment Counselor
Similar to the banker, an investment advisor will provide a final valuation of invested assets, and work with lawyer and accountant to determine how to transfer ownership or to liquidate investments.

Every Estate Is Unique

Just as grief is not the same between two people, neither is an estate. While it is valuable for you to ask others about their experiences with professionals, remember that every single estate is unique. Just because the woman you play bridge with on Tuesday mornings had a nightmare of an accountant doesn't mean the same will happen to you. Your situation may not involve all the professionals I've mentioned. You want to find those who will comfort you and protect you, and your children, from much of the complexities and demands that come at a time like this. May God grant you the grace to face this difficult new beginning, as you face life on your own.

When Your Husband Leaves You on Your Own

"'I hate divorce,' says the Lord God of Israel" (Malachi 2:16). So do you, you say. The dissolution of a marriage brings awful disruption and hurtful consequence. And well it should; it is the breaking of a bond, of a lifetime commitment. It is loyalty betrayed. There are times, however, when reconciliation is not possible or prudent. Such issues as alcoholism, homosexuality, abandonment, imprisonment, serious neurotic conditions, and adultery may be just cause for dissolution. The *Encyclopedia of Biblical and Christian Ethics* puts it this way:

> There is no warrant in Scripture to submit to such evils. In some cases spiritual heroism on the part of a suffering spouse may be redemptive.
>
> Where redemptive steps prove fruitless, most Christians understand the Scriptures to allow merciful escape from such evils.[1]

If reconciliation is not possible, the marriage is dissolved, and should be done so in accord with safeguards for both parties and their children.

The burden to deal justly is great in a divorce. Communication, which is usually strained and difficult, is most important. I've walked in your shoes. It is not a good time.

Tea *Time!*

Are you *sure* you can't work things out?

What to Do

If you are in the midst of a divorce, you should immediately:

1. *Establish your own savings and credit.*
2. *Make an inventory of all tangible and intangible assets.*
3. *Hire an attorney.* Just as I'd go to a criminal lawyer if I were in trouble with the law, or an estate lawyer if I wanted to set up my estate, so I would find a lawyer who was practiced in divorce court if I were getting a divorce. And I would shop price. Once I found a lawyer I felt comfortable with, I would ask for a written statement that put a cap on the fee.

   The lawyer should guide you through the emotional train wreck of divorce, and guard your interest, as well as meet all the legal requirements.

   If no children are involved, and if there is no property to speak of, your state may allow you to petition the court yourself. This is risky business, considering that the future holds unexpected turns. Suppose *you* do well in life, and your ex decides *he* wants a piece of the pie?

   - Check with your attorney first, but you may want to *close joint charge accounts or notify businesses that one or the other will be removed from the account.*
   - Once again, you should check with your attorney first, but you may want to *freeze all bank and investment accounts, or give instructions that no transaction may take place without written approval of both parties.*
   - *Keep cool. The more hostility and bickering, the higher the*

cost of divorce. Stand your ground. Ask yourself, *How will this settlement/alimony affect me when I am sixty-five?*

- *Consult an attorney to rewrite your will.*
- *Get to know the divorce laws of your state.* Check with your public library to find laws governing your state. Some states are called *community property states.* That means the state recognizes all property accumulated during the marriage to belong equally to husband and wife. This does not necessarily mean each gets half. (Only some of the community property states require a fifty-fifty split.) What seems to be emerging as the critical question, though, is "Half of *what?*"

Other states are called *separate property states,* and assume that property accumulated during the marriage, as well as gifts and inheritances received during the marriage, are considered separate property and are not divided at the time of divorce.

There are also *kitchen sink states,* wherein separate property and assets owned before the marriage are divisible, no matter when or how they were acquired. Some kitchen sink states will divide property less evenly if a special need is demonstrated.

A judge will consider certain factors:

- Whether any property belonged to one of you before marriage.
- Whether any property that was acquired during the marriage was a gift to one of you specifically.
- Whether any property that was acquired during the marriage was inherited by one of you specifically.
- Whether any property was acquired by exchanging one of the above.

- The length of the marriage, not to mention the age and health of each spouse.
- The financial condition of each spouse, including such things as income, education, occupation, training, and employability.
- Each person's specific contribution to the acquisition of the property, as well as each person's contribution to the preservation or appreciation of the property.

There is a shift taking place in courts across America, however, and marriage is being redefined. At one time, marriage was not viewed as a joint venture; when the marriage dissolved, property was split according to who held title. It is from this concept that alimony sprang, which was something the main property owner (usually the husband) "gave" the wife.

According to Maggie Mahar, in her article "Splitsville," "The latest trend in divorce law [is that] the spouse who shares equally in the risks of a marriage should share equally in the spoils—even if the marriage eventually fails."[2] Mahar continues, stating that it's up to the judge "to say whether 'equitable' means 'equal.' In other words, is a wife who stays at home to raise children an equal partner in the joint venture of a marriage?"[3]

What Is at Stake in Divorce?

For Christians, our witness is at stake. Whether we like it or not, if we have proclaimed Jesus Christ as our Lord and Master, the world watches us. It is incumbent upon us to demonstrate fidelity to the Word of God. Though your marriage may be in shambles, it is still necessary for you to exhibit grace and Christian behavior. Christian behavior, however, *does not* include staying put if you (and your children) are being battered!

There are other issues at stake, such as custody of children, child support, alimony, division of property.

Custody of children. This is such a tragic issue! As a child of divorce, and as a mother who once divorced, I understand the profound emotional complications experienced by children of divorce. Custody issues can be highly charged, so consult an attorney to protect the children's interest. Will there be joint custody, visitation rights, restraining orders? Who will pay for travel if the children have to visit a parent in a faraway town?

Child support. Until what age will the children be supported? Will your husband assist in extracurricular expenses, trips, medical care outside of standard insurance coverage, college education? Who will pay for health insurance for the children? Who will benefit from the tax deduction?

Because of noncompliance of child support, most states are cracking down on deadbeat dads, and have established child support administration agencies. Congress passed the *Family Support Act of 1988,* which enforced child support orders. If you are having difficulty obtaining child support due, there are agencies that will help you:

- FOCUS (For Children and Us) is a nonprofit group of professionals. Call (212) 693-1655.
- National Child Support Enforcement Association, Hall of the States, Suite 613, 444 N Capitol St. NW, Washington, DC 20001. Call (202) 624-8180.

- EXPOSE (for military spouses), P.O. Box 11191, Alexandria, VA 22312. Call (703) 941-5844 (day); (703) 255-2917 (night).
- National Domestic Violence Hotline. Call 1-800-555-1212 for their toll-free number.

Alimony. In *Money Demons,* Dr. Susan Forward warns women that an upset husband might use money as a weapon. She says:

> The desire to escape the emotional battering of a bitter divorce frequently causes women to lose sight of their financial interests.... Money (and the things it can buy) is all too often a vindictive husband's weapon of choice for acting out feelings of hurt or anger when a relationship breaks up. [4]

Speaking for myself, when I faced leaving my first husband (we both had biblical grounds, though it was before I became a Christian), I was frozen with fear about money. Where would it come from? How would I survive? What should I demand? Could I demand anything? Help!

Since the advent of no-fault divorce, much of the focus has switched to custody rights and distribution of assets. Alimony seems to be going the way of the Model T, yet there are still some alimony settlements in divorce. Alimony will stop, once you remarry, and taxes must be paid, since it is considered income rather than a distribution or "settlement" of property. Some women are offered a lump-sum settlement, either in cash or in real or personal property.

When considering alimony or a lump sum, be sure to consider the following:

1. *Alimony can be written with an escalation clause, or you may petition the court for an increase in the amount you receive.* (This would commonly happen if your ex-husband's assets increased dramatically. The reverse is true, by the way; your husband can petition the court to get alimony reduced if he can prove you are making an income on your own!) *Note:* There is such a thing as an alimony trust. This is of particular interest to people in high tax brackets, and requires the savvy of a good attorney.

2. *Taxes are not paid on a settlement.*

3. *If you take a lump sum, you are guaranteed the amount and can invest it.* (However, if your former husband's assets increase dramatically, too bad for you. Too bad for you, also, if you do not manage the lump sum well.)

Property division. Consider tax liability as well as upkeep when consenting to property division. Who gets what is an important issue in divorce, and you will want to be certain you aren't saddling yourself with future debt or responsibility. For instance, don't presume that rental property is a good deal unless you are fully aware of the cost of upkeep, property taxes, and the hassles of being a landlord. Is he leaving you a car that still has payments, is a gas guzzler, costs a lot to insure, and breaks down often? Yippee, skippee.

Tax laws change *all the time.* If you are transferring ownership from one to the other, or from joint to individual ownership, be certain beforehand that you understand any potential capital gains liability.

Pensions and Social Security. The law says you are entitled to a share of your husband's pension plans, most especially if you've been married a long while. If your marriage lasted at least ten years, you may also receive some of your ex-spouse's Social Security benefits upon his retirement or death.

Existing debt. A crucial factor in a divorce settlement is who will bear responsibility for existing debt. According to *The Divorce Decision Workbook,* your creditors do not care one whit how your separation or divorce agreement divides responsibility for debt. You are each liable for the full amount of debt on joint credit cards until the bill is paid. [5]

Keep in mind that if the charge accounts you used with your husband were contracted jointly, you will both have the same credit history. Before the final decree is signed, make sure that all joint accounts are paid off, closed, and new accounts started in your individual names.

Be careful not to run up charge account debt as retaliation. If it can later be proven that is exactly what you did, you may end up footing the bill yourself.

Money and Thee: Finding Your Way

Whether grieving the death of your marriage, or the death of your husband, the world keeps turning. Bill collectors, children's concerns, legal matters, and taxes continue to demand your involvement. This is an emotionally draining time for you, sister, but if you are left on your own, no one can walk this new path for you. Others may stand by to offer a hand, but there are only two certain guarantees that will brace you as you go: God's perfect grace, and time. May his grace be abundant as your journey alone begins.

Now it's your turn to write. Think about what you have read in this chapter. How does it apply to you? Soul-search a little, and jot down your thoughts.

Where I am now: _____

_____

_____

Where I'd like to be: _____

_____

_____

A Few Important Questions

- Who continues the mortgage payment? Children are best served if they stay in their own home. If the mortgage is retired, who pays for taxes, insurance, upkeep?
- Can you remain beneficiary on his life insurance policy? You may request that you be named an irrevocable beneficiary, which means you cannot be removed as beneficiary without your written permission. You will also be notified if the policy is in danger of lapse.
- Will the kids be covered on his health insurance policy? Can your coverage continue for a while, or will he pay for you to obtain your own coverage?
- Can you claim one or two kids as dependents, even though he wants to claim the children for income tax purposes?
- Who will pay the attorney fees? If he doesn't pay your attorney fee (but said he would) are you then liable?

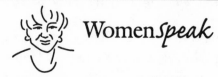 Women *Speak*

"Not only is she still in shock that he dropped dead, she has to sell his pick-up truck just to get the money to bury him!"

———

"It's so sad. All he ever talked about was leaving his place to his granddaughter. Why on earth didn't he update his will?"

———

"It was an absolute nightmare! When my mother moved to an apartment after Dad died, she threw away tons of important papers. We had to start from scratch and do a lot of guessing."

———

"When Dad died, the IRS valued his business at ten times more than we thought it was worth. The tax was $397,000. We had to sell everything to pay the tax."

———

"The smartest thing every woman can do to protect herself financially is to be a full partner with her husband. Be certain he has sufficient term life insurance to protect you and your children during the most vulnerable years."

———

"The smartest thing every woman can do to protect herself financially is: get involved with the finances. I once knew a woman who was older, and all of her life her husband took care of everything, from balancing the checkbook to buying tires for the car. When he died, she knew nothing about the real world, leaving greedy relatives to take over her checkbook. They left her with nothing, and literally spent all of her money."

———

"Get a written retainer agreement [from your lawyer.] Make sure it is understood. Many, many clients get scalped in probate. Probate is usually very clean, very simple, and is performed mostly by a paralegal."

ten

The State of Your Estate

I met Caroline at a retreat. Her story was not new to me; I just filed it under the category "Nothing surprises me anymore." Caroline was married for twenty-five years when her husband died. Since their two children were grown and self-supporting, she and her husband assumed that Caroline would inherit her husband's estate, which wasn't much to begin with. Wrong. Since he died intestate (without a will), the courts split the estate; half to the grown children, half to Caroline.

Did Caroline's children come to the rescue? Nope. They added to her grief. One son was married, and Caroline's daughter-in-law had ideas for her husband's "rightful share" of the estate. The other son was eager to get his share, to support a chemical abuse problem.

Caroline didn't have any fight in her. She barely gets by now, working as a clerk in an all-night convenience store.

It happens all the time, and there are variations to Caroline's experience. State laws dictate what percentage of someone's estate the spouse, *and in some cases,* the children receive ... even if a will is left behind!

What is an estate in the first place? In a nutshell, an estate is the sum total of all the assets and liabilities a person leaves behind at death. Assets can include personal belongings, real estate, investments, insurance, even potential earnings (as in the case of a writer whose books might continue to sell).

Liabilities will include any indebtedness and, in many cases, contractual obligations.

While I will emphasize the importance of having an estate *plan*, we must discuss other factors that influence the distribution of someone's estate, such as probate procedures and taxes. Let's start with probate, and end with taxes, with a lot of helpful information in between.

What You Need to Know About Probate

Probate simply refers to the public administration of all your assets and liabilities at the time of your death. Not all estates are required to be probated, depending upon how property is owned, and what the value of it is. Every state has different laws (for instance, in our state, most modest estates do not go to probate). Probate can also be used to test the validity of your will. Any assets with beneficiaries, such as insurance policies or retirement accounts, automatically avoid probate.

Probate costs can sometimes be unrealistically high. Some states allow lawyers to charge a percentage of the gross estate. You avoid probate problems by having your affairs in order, which means you have a rock-solid will and a trust in place.

Here are some ways to avoid probate problems:

1. *Joint tenancy with rights of survivorship.* This is the most commonly used method to avoid probate. In this case, two or more owners must hold equal shares to qualify as joint tenants, and assets held this way cannot be willed to anyone else. There are three drawbacks to joint tenancy with rights of survivorship:

- If you add a nonspousal co-owner, you could be liable for gift tax.

- A joint tenant could jeopardize your property.
- When the last owner dies, the probate protection is gone.

2. *Multiple party accounts with financial institutions.* This is called a Payable on Death arrangement (POD). This is a cost-free option. You simply list a beneficiary on all your banking signature cards.

3. *Uniform Transfer on Death designations* (TOD). Many states offer these simplified transfers, which allow for securities to bypass probate by naming beneficiaries on stocks, bonds, and so on. Some states allow transfer on death to designated beneficiaries for such things as automobiles and boats.

Summary Probate

Every state has its version of a "small" estate. If you've reduced your estate through wise designation of beneficiaries, gifts, and the like, you may still have some estate left to probate. In a *summary probate*, the executor files a form asking for the simplified probate procedure. This is less costly, takes less time, and is often done by mail.

You may be lucky to live in a state that has adopted a simplified probate process under the Uniform Probate Code. Simplified probate is an informal procedure, usually involves no court hearing, and cuts down significantly on the cost and delay of probate.

Suppose an estate gets probated. What determines the things that are included in an estate? It all becomes a matter of control over an asset, or *ownership*.

Ownership

The absolute, bottom line about what gets included in an estate revolves around ownership. If there is the slightest hint that you could have control over something, even if you no longer have that something in your possession, and exert no control over it, the *hint* of control constitutes ownership. Why does this matter? *Ownership constitutes inclusion in your gross estate for tax purposes.* For example:

- A husband names his wife beneficiary of his insurance policy, but he retains ownership of the policy. Even though the wife gets a death benefit, proceeds are included in his gross estate, since he still has the right to change beneficiary because he is the owner of the policy ... ownership.

- A mother sets up a bank account (or CD or mutual fund or stock portfolio) for her teenage son, who has the responsibility to manage the funds. Mom's name is on the account, even though she makes no claim to the money. Her name is on the account ... ownership.

- A husband leaves the house to his wife—absolutely, positively—unless she remarries, at which time the house goes to the children. Because of the stipulation, he still has say (even after he is dead!), so the value of the house is included in his estate ... ownership.

If this sounds convoluted, it is! The bottom line: If anyone has the slightest control over any property, contracts, finances (even if through a will), any value will be included in the final estate, for tax purposes.

Note: Probate can really get confusing if a business is involved. If you (or your husband) share in the ownership of a business, consider a buy-sell agreement. This agreement will pass legal ownership of the business to remaining partner(s), or others decided upon before death, without business disruption. (Whether the business even continues to exist may depend on a carefully drafted buy-sell.) A buy-sell will also evaluate the worth of the business beforehand, and the IRS may stick with that evaluation. It is utterly critical that such an agreement be devised by a professional, since buy-sell agreements can create the complexity and confusion against which they should be insuring.

There is much to the business of dying. It is regrettable that we have to put so much energy into legally protecting our heirs from claims by others, and into legally protecting our assets from tax burdens. Threats to your estate can be met head-on with a good plan.

State Your Plans for Your Estate

Many people don't think it's necessary to make a plan for what happens to their estate when they die. But without some kind of plan, you could inadvertently disinherit loved ones, and create havoc in the lives of those left behind.

Too young to bother with this, you say? Not so fast! You are never too young to die. According to Sherman Smith, author of *Put Your Money Where Your Heart Is*, everyone needs an estate plan. Dr. Smith believes that if you have any assets at all, you need estate planning. He carries his advice farther than one would expect, but with good sense:

> I consider my family as an asset. We all would place more value in our children than we would in our stock portfolio, or in our house, wouldn't we? To me, if you have $25 to your name, and two kids, you have a need to do estate planning.[1]

An estate plan is a highly personal review and plan to protect or pass along your estate. (Once again, your estate is the sum total of your tangible and intangible assets and liabilities at the time of your death.) An estate plan can also preserve your standard of living, as well as preserve your capital assets while you are alive.

Often mistakenly believed to be reserved for the well-to-do, an estate plan is a formal (and often legal) document that spells out how you want your estate distributed to rightful heirs, or to protect heirs (and minor children) in the event of your death. This sounds like a will, doesn't it? There is a difference. Look at it this way: A will tells the state *who* gets what; a good estate plan makes sure they *get* the "what," without the "what" being diminished by such things as taxes or unscrupulous or inexperienced administration.

To help you further understand the difference between an estate plan and a will, think back to chapter two and business plans. When we discussed having a business plan, we first had to have a mission statement or objective, followed by a specific plan, followed by action, followed by review. Apply that principle to an estate plan. Call the estate plan your **mission statement**—a comprehensive consideration of *all aspects of estate transfer* to designated beneficiaries. Your will becomes part of your specific **plan**—it specifies who will receive what, and designates an administrator (executor). The **action** (disposition of your estate) will take place in an orderly and prescribed manner, once you have passed on. With the help of an estate planning expert, the **review** is an ongoing process while you are still alive.

A good estate plan will include instructions about the following:

- The care and rearing of children and dependents
- Taxes, which are a huge consideration with some estates. There are many, many tax traps that swallow personal estates whole—in one big gulp!—and could have been avoided under the counsel and guidance of an experienced estate planner.
- Personal wishes with regard to as the distribution of assets, liquidation of estate, care of surviving spouse.
- How to pay debts. An estate plan should provide enough liquid funds to pay immediate debts. Debts against the estate must be brought to some kind of resolution when the property holder dies. Unless proper plans have been laid, in some states, bank accounts can be frozen at time of death, and safe deposit boxes sealed. (You certainly don't want your heirs to pay your debts themselves! Or, most commonly, be forced into selling part of your estate for quick cash to pay for final expenses, medical bills, or debts against the estate. We've all seen newspaper ads in the classifieds: "*Forced estate sale.*" Forced sales, by the way, are often the result of an estate in which the assets were comprised mostly of real estate, and therefore there was no cash on hand.)
  - Your estate plan should also include documents with provisions that will meet your needs, *should you need care during your lifetime.*

The two legal documents most used when creating an estate plan are wills and trusts. You can create an estate plan without drawing up a trust, but it would be folly to leave your heirs without the assurance of a will. Many people regard a well-constructed will as adequate, and do not feel the need for a formal estate plan.

Writing Your Will

Do you have an updated will at this moment? If not, join the crowd! Past presidents, judges, businessmen, lawyers, accountants, and celebrities have died intestate, which means "without a will." Many people today think they either don't need a will or they will "one day get around to it." This is a serious blunder, especially if a surviving spouse or children are involved. Let me tell you why.

A will expresses your wishes for the distribution of what you leave behind. If you die intestate, the probate laws of your state kick in. That means an impersonal judge will make the decisions *you* should have made: who gets your kids, what portion of your estate will go to your spouse, who gets the house, the car, whether your second-cousin twice removed (the one you really, really don't like) gets a piece of your estate pie. Incidentally, state laws vary as to the percentage of estate the surviving spouse should receive. And in some states, children are entitled to a certain percentage, regardless of the provisions in the will.

If you die without a will, you will leave an unfair burden upon your heirs, who now have to go through a legal and sometimes expensive rigmarole to access your estate.

Tea *Time!*

Make a cup of strong tea. Now personalize the issue of estate planning. Ask yourself: Who will care for my children if my husband and I are killed in a car crash tomorrow morning? My mother? My mother-in-law? My sister? My sister-in-law? Foster care? Will there be a custody battle? How will my death affect my children? Don't I owe it to them to make provision for them if I'm not here?

When you are ready to write your will, you need to *get thee to a lawyer!* Yes, there are do-it-yourself will kits on the market, but you are risking too much if you trust yourself, or some computer software, to protect your estate. Don't make the mistake of thinking any written document to transfer property will be accepted by the courts. The fee for a will is usually small in comparison to the peace of mind you will attain. Call different law firms and inquire about their fees. Don't be afraid to shop for professional service.

When you meet with your lawyer, bring as much information as you can: names and birth dates of dependents; name of the person who has agreed to be legal guardian to your children in the event of your death (as well as a secondary choice); all heirs you wish to be included in your estate distribution; information about all tangible and intangible assets; information about insurance policies; your Social Security number; all data about current and previous marriages; tax information; Armed Forces records; information on any business owned; list of debts or liabilities; information about safe deposit boxes or vaults; requests for burial and funeral.

If you have a will, it may need to be updated. Many factors come to play throughout life that can alter the will you drew up years ago. Those factors could even cause the will to be considered invalid. For example:

- Are your children grown? Do you have more children to consider, or have you lost a child?
- Yippee! You're a grandma!
- You no longer have many assets (or liabilities), or you have much more than when you wrote your will.
- You have moved to another state (*big* consideration!), and the laws of the new state make the old will invalid. This is

where a knowledgeable lawyer is important: If you have moved to a new state, *the state you left may have claim to your estate.*

- Heirs or beneficiaries may have died, or you no longer wish to bequeath to them.
- The witnesses to your signature on the original will may not be alive, or cannot be located.
- Your executor is no longer capable of overseeing your estate, or may not be acceptable under the laws of your state. An executor (executrix) is the person designated in the will to oversee the terms of the will. In other words, he or she becomes the "manager" of what was left behind.

Selecting an Executor

Being an executor or personal representative to an estate is a huge responsibility. More often than not, the husband names the wife executrix, and vice versa. Some estate planning professionals advise against this. The demands are simply too great to bear during the grieving process, and the demands will not wait. For instance, the federal government expects payment of any taxes due within nine months of death.

Be sure that whoever you pick as executor is not only willing to shoulder the responsibility, but is able. This can be a formidable responsibility! The executor must literally represent you, after you have died. Someone once wrote a list of possible duties of an executor, and the list filled an entire page! Suffice to say, the executor's job includes such things as following specific instructions for your burial; making certain minor children are placed in the care of named guardians; making an inventory of the safe deposit box; assessing the status of all your bank accounts; canceling credit card accounts; locating and describing *all* property you may own; finding all life insurance policies; finding the best markets for properties you own; contacting and working with all pertinent professionals (stockbroker, lawyer, accountant, Realtor, banker); contacting all previous employers should there be a death benefit or vested pension; paying bills; collecting debts; and on and on.

Some professionals feel it is best to appoint a bank official as executor. They claim that the cost is worth the time involved. Others rarely name a bank or "corporate individual" as personal representative, claiming that they are cumbersome to work with and charge exorbitant fees. Call your bank and ask what their fee would be.

It is common to formalize yet another legal document when in the process of writing your will, and that is a power of attorney, which, in a sense, gets "tacked on" to your will. A power of attorney makes good sense.

Giving Someone Power of Attorney

A power of attorney is a legal document that gives someone (usually a spouse) the right to act on behalf of someone who is absent, or unable to act for himself. In the absence of a power of attorney, the courts will step in and administrate for you.

Many people draw up a power of attorney when they reach their twilight years and want the comfort and certainty of a trusted friend or relative tending their affairs, should they become too feeble. However, there is a big difference between authorizing someone to sign on your bank account, and putting them on the account as a joint account holder. If you designate someone power of attorney, you are merely giving that person the right to sign. They must have your consent. (A *durable* power of attorney means that person can sign on your account, should you be disabled and unable to give consent, but only according to the terms and stipulations of the legal document giving that person power of attorney.) The bank needs to see a copy of the document in order to allow the person to sign.

On the other hand, if you simply put someone on your account, making it a joint account, you may have inadvertently created an estate problem. What happens to the money in the account when you die? It becomes the rightful property of the other person listed on the account. Hold it, you say! You didn't intend for your son to get all the money; you wanted it shared between all three of your children. Oops. The same situation happens, by the way, when parents put the "family farm" in the name of one of their children to avoid probate. Parents die. That one child gets the house. But you wanted all the kids to get the farm. Oops again.

If you are engaged in writing a formal estate plan, and have already drafted your will, and included a power of attorney, your estate planner may suggest you consider a trust. This may all seem like a lot of bother, but if you have assets (and children) to protect, read on.

Setting Up a Trust

What is a trust? It is a legal contract that transfers assets to a trustee (which could be you, another person, or a company), who then manages the assets on behalf of those named in the trust as beneficiaries. A trust is a separate and distinct entity unto itself. It controls the assets or property for the benefit of those named. A trust, when set up properly, can protect an estate from taxes. But if the maker of the trust has *any* control over the trust (ownership) it becomes taxable.

Many people name a bank or a trust company as trustee. There are a couple of good reasons for this. The trust is usually better managed by professionals than by an individual. Also, if there is misappropriation by a bank employee, the bank will stand behind the loss. There are also some reasons why *not* to do this: Banks, trust companies, and corporate trustees will not usually become involved if the account is less than $50,000 or $100,000. Also, they usually charge high fees for trust management.

A trust can be established at any time and for various reasons. For example:

- A husband setting up a trust for his wife.
- Parents setting up a trust for minor children.
- Parents setting up a trust for a mentally or physically challenged child.
- An older woman who sets up a trust for herself, because she no longer wants the responsibility of handling her own affairs. (This example, and the next, are examples of a trust created during a person's lifetime, which can be different from what is commonly peddled as a "living trust.")
- A busy woman who does not have the energy or time to handle her affairs, so she sets up a trust to take care of them for her (I'm told this is not uncommon for world-famous authors ... OK, and for world-famous editors, too!).

There are two kinds of trusts: *revocable trusts*—you can change or nullify the trust at any time—and *irrevocable trusts*.

This trust is in cement and cannot be changed once it is established.

There is also such a thing as a living trust, which is a popular concept that has appealed to many people. One reason for its popularity is the tremendous marketing strategy of the peddlers of these trusts. A living trust is not always what it's cracked up to be.

Living Trusts

What a living trust will *not* do:

- It will not change your estate or inheritance taxes. (A properly set up "bypass trust" can help those with high estate values to avoid federal estate taxes.)
- It will not save income tax during your lifetime; any income will be taxed.
- It will *not* replace a will. (When a will is in place, along with a trust, it is called a "pour-over will." The "pour-over" provision in your will leaves all of your nontrust assets to your trust.)
- It will not guarantee an easy settlement if the estate is complicated to begin with.

A living trust operates during the lifetime of the grantor (person who makes the trust). It is the opposite of a *testamentary trust*, which is a trust created in your will. Probably the most important reason for a living trust is to arrange for someone to take over your affairs if you become incapacitated or mentally incapable. This is different from a power of attorney, which does not change title or ownership, but merely gives someone the right to sign his or her name on your accounts. A trustee has authority over property and affairs according to the terms of the trust.

A living trust provides a way to keep your assets out of harm's way should you become unable to manage them properly. Under a living trust, you can name yourself as the trustee (person who manages the trust), as well as appoint a successor trustee (person who manages the trust in your behalf if you die or can no longer manage yourself). If you have a living trust at the time of your death, your assets are usually not subject to probate when you die, because your estate continues under the management of your successor trustee. (*Take Note!* If you are the sole trustee, and you die or become incapacitated, the court will have to administer your trust.)

Since you are both the maker of the trust (grantor) and the trustee, you can stipulate anything you like in the terms of the trust, and if it is revocable, you can change the terms when you wish. For instance, you might state that upon your death, your assets will be divided equally among three children. You might attach a spendthrift clause to the terms insofar as that certain son of yours is concerned, to protect his inheritance from claims by creditors. (One creative father brought home the admonition "Get a job!" when he left his son one dollar for every dollar the son earned through gainful employment.) You may want to distribute income according to a certain schedule, or you may want to state that, should your childless daughter die before the trust is allocated, the proceeds revert back to the trust rather than going to her husband (or her husband's family).

Caution! Living trust sales are a growing area of consumer fraud, and most people who put their money in a fraudulent trust never see it again. Be wary of mail or telephone solicitation, "free" seminars or workshops (check these out first!), and advertisements. Some living trusts are sold as part of an entire "estate planning portfolio," and while some of them are good, some of them are not. Many states are enacting legislation to require that most "living trust" salespeople be licensed.

Also, the cost of creating and administrating a living trust might outweigh the benefits to you. If you are convinced you should have a living trust, it should be drafted by someone with knowledge of your state's law. Consult with an experienced estate planner, estate lawyer, or estate accountant.

Besides wanting to distribute your estate in an orderly and equitable manner, one compelling reason for plans and wills and trusts is the looming presence of the tax man—a grim reaper if there ever was one!

The Tax Man Cometh

I am cautious to say too much about tax matters at time of death, for a couple of reasons. First, I am not a tax expert by any stretch of the imagination, and second, tax laws seem to be changing faster than you can reheat pizza in the microwave! Having said that, here is a brief tax primer:

You are not obliged to pay *income tax* on an inheritance unless it was a tax-deferred investment such as a pension or IRA. However, you might have to pay a federal *estate tax*, and it can be a bone-crusher, taxing anywhere from 37 percent to 65 percent of the estate. (And this does not count state estate tax, inheritance tax, generation skipping tax, or excise taxes on pensions, breathing tax...just kidding!) The federal estate tax considers *every*thing you pass to heirs.

At this writing, there are two exceptions to this tax:

1. *The Unified Credit Allowance* reduces estate and gift tax

by $192,800, which is the equivalent of reducing taxable gifts and estate by $600,000. The Unified Credit Allowance gives every single person this reduction tax-free. If your combined assets exceed $600,000, *including future appreciation*, then you might want to set up a "Family Trust," and separate your unified credit. For instance, suppose my books make the *New York Times* best-seller list, way off in the distant future (be still, my heart!). If I die, the revenuer will appraise my earning *potential* through continuing royalties and add that amount to the total estate evaluation. This is where a knowledgeable attorney comes in.

2. *The Unlimited Marital Deduction* allows assets to pass between spouses with no federal gift or estate tax liability. The marital deduction will not apply if a joint will between husband and wife is in effect, because the surviving spouse is not receiving a transfer of assets to do with as she chooses, she is receiving the property according to a preexisting formula.

The Tax Man Cometh and Cometh

So you have the Unlimited Marital Deduction and you are all set, right? Not so fast. What happens when you die? As I said, when someone dies, *everything* is valued for tax purposes, and estate taxes can be mighty high. Let's suppose your husband left you an estate of $500,000. No taxes. Nice and clean. Well, with some good investments, with the fact that your condo has gone up in value in the past few years, and with the life insurance proceeds that kick in when you die, your estate is now worth $1,000,000. According to the 1998 tax tables, your kids will have to come up with $155,460 for estate taxes within nine months. If you had recognized the possible tax consequence in advance, and jockeyed your assets around under the direction of a competent estate planner, the kids might not be scurrying to sell the condo.

The government will put a value on everything that can be valued monetarily, such as:

- Bank accounts, including money markets
- Securities, including mutual funds
- Bonds
- Contents of safe deposit box
- Qualified pension plans and annuities
- Cash
- Real estate, including your home
- Royalties, or any other income
- Business interests
- Tangible personal property, including such things as art, jewelry, guns, cars
- Inheritances or trusts
- Life insurance (death benefit, if you are the insured; cash value, if you are the owner)

Tea *Time!*

Evaluate the tax burden on your heirs. If you are currently married, evaluate estate tax as if you are widowed. Consider all assets, including potential values, as would the IRS. To whom are you leaving your legacy?

Money and Thee: Guiding Your Way

The intent of this chapter was to cause you just enough concern to look into your specific situation. *I have to do the same thing myself!* Yes, Joe and I have a will—a good will—with all the bells and whistles that a smart lawyer knows we need in order to distribute our assets as we wish. Writing this chapter has made me think. What if Joe and I are killed in a car wreck? Sure, we're leaving Josh and Molly the house, and the cars, and the insurance. What does all that add up to? And are all the necessary papers easily accessible? Are all of our records up to date? What kind of burden would we be placing on Josh as executor (he lives 2,700 miles away from us) if something happened today … or tomorrow … or next month?

You see, estate planning is about caring so much for those whom you are leaving behind that you want to make things as clean and clear as possible. And I believe there are far too many rules, loopholes, and tax demands, for you to be able to draft your plan without help. If the only help you get is a book from the library on estate planning, it's a start.

We've walked a long way on this journey toward financial stability, haven't we? Let's turn a corner now and walk through a nice neighborhood, and look at all the pretty houses. Wouldn't you like one of them to be yours?

Now it's your turn to write. Think about what you have read in this chapter. How does it apply to you? Soul-search a little, and jot down your thoughts.

Where I am now: _____

Where I'd like to be: _____

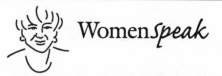

Women*speak*

"The biggest mistake I ever made when it comes to money is believing an architect who said we could build our first home for X amount of dollars, and then not getting a firm bid on all the work. He was off by 20 percent. This was in 1981, when interest rates were 18 percent."

———

"Buyers who 'want a deal' are the ones who go to 'For Sale by Owner' homes."

———

"Shop for a mortgage. A buyer needs to compare the interest rate and cost of a loan to really compare loan companies. Get good faith estimates in writing, and compare APR rates."

———

"When entering a buy-sell agreement, make sure there is a back door before you go in the front door."

———

"You'd swear he was running out to buy a loaf of bread. Put my husband within sniffing distance of a new car—a drive on a car lot is terminal—and he turns into a crazy man. Do they, like, spray the seats with testosterone or something?"

———

"I used to think, If I can afford the monthly payment, I can buy the car. I never considered the overall cost, the interest, stuff like that. When I married my husband and we were negotiating with a dealer for a new car, I asked, 'Can you get the payment down to around two hundred dollars a month?' I thought my husband would have a fit and fall in it. I've since learned: that is not how to bargain for a car!"

eleven

The Mortgage and the Car Payment: Two Certainties in Life!

Well, here we are in the "home" stretch. Before I rev up my engines and speed into this chapter on home and car buying, I want to share something that happened to us while I was writing this book: We sold our cabin on the lake (are you ready for this?) because we couldn't afford to keep up with expenses.

"What? You're writing an entire book on money management, and now you tell us you were having trouble making ends meet, yourself?"

Before you ask for your money back, listen to my story. Remember that sometimes—for reasons outside of themselves—good people end up living beyond their means. That is what happened to us. Several factors figured in. For one, we lived on lake property that has dramatically increased in value over the years (as one friend put it, "They don't make more lakefront!"). Property taxes have increased right along with property value, to the point that our latest assessment put our tax bill at over 10 percent of our monthly income. Not a good place to be!

Concurrent with the property tax increase was discovery of a heart ailment that took me out of active employment and catapulted medical expenses into thousands of dollars, in spite of savings and insurance. I can say unequivocally that had Joseph and I *not* been frugal and careful with money management, we would have faced our crisis long before that moment.

We convened a family meeting and came to a single conclusion: It was time to sell. The sale of our lakefront property would enable us to pay every penny due, as well as purchase a different home—one with much lower taxes, I might add! It was a wrenching decision. We had to abandon dreams of our grandchildren growing up on the lake, dreams of living there forever. Clinging stubbornly to those dreams would have sent us careening headfirst into a bottomless pit. It was a hard decision, but we made it prayerfully, and it was the right decision.

Tea *Time!*

Are you living in a home that forces you to live above your means? Are you a slave to a mortgage, to taxes, to upkeep? Please accept my two cents right now and prayerfully consider moving to a ... shall I say ... less taxing place to call your own.

OR

Is it time to upgrade or downsize?

Has your family grown, or have the babes left the nest?

Because of our experience, I've spent a lot of time in a Realtor's office. The "rush" of making an offer on another home, the anxiety of waiting for a response, the agony of decision over any counteroffers, and the thrill of hearing our Realtor say, "It's a deal!" are all fresh memories for me. Since buying a home is not something many of us do too often during a lifetime, I felt it important to include some information regarding this in my book. Here goes.

What Should You Look for When Buying a Home?

When you are buying a home, there are a few practical things to consider.

Room sizes. Arm yourself with your faithful spiral notebook and a measuring tape. (If you are selling, a layout of rooms for prospective buyers would be helpful.) Consider all of the rooms. Think of your furniture, your kids, your pets, when you think about the home layout.

Everything technical. Does the home you are interested in have septic, or city sewer? Does it have natural gas heat, or depend on a relic of a wood stove in the basement? Is the electrical service adequate and up to code? Check plumbing, wiring, insulation, roof, parking, etc.

What comes with the home. Make certain every single thing that should be included or excluded is written down. For instance, light fixtures are normally considered an attached part of the home, and should stay. In several cases, though, people have invested money into a light fixture (or it has been handed down from a great-aunt) and they want to take it with them. If this is the case, it should be noted in the buy-sell agreement.

Quality of life at your new home. Are there nearby churches, schools, or parks? Is shopping convenient? How will you get your mail? Will your pets have a place to run, or to relieve themselves? Is there an all-night disco down the street that has loud music on weekends?

Should You Buy or Sell a Home Without the Help of a Realtor?

Ever hear the Latin phrase *caveat emptor?* Let the buyer beware. You may be able to strike a fine deal on your own. You might also end up buying a can of worms, if the seller did not disclose something about the house. If you are selling your home on your own, chances are you will lose money. Take the case of Sue and Charlie:

Sue and Charlie decided to sell their home without the help of a Realtor. They had "heard" what their neighbor sold his house for, and put a value on their own home that was above market value. The home sat on the market for many months. Oh, they did everything they could to generate interest: open houses, signs, ads in the paper. When they finally went to a qualified agent, they learned the area was in a down market and they had overpriced their home. For the six months the house just sat, it cost them taxes, insurance, maintenance, and upkeep. So, when they did list with an agent, they ended up with less *than they most likely would have received had they listed it in the first place.*

You will serve yourself well if you work with a real estate agent. But not just any agent! Many fine people in real estate sales are amateurs. Sorry. This is big business. Go to a pro. As Maurice Dubois says in his excellent book, *Home Buyer's Confidential,* "A home is too large an asset to allow someone with little education or experience to help you."[1]

When you are ready to enlist a Realtor, here are some things to look for:

- *Experience.* Ask how long the person has been in business and whether it has been full-time or part-time.
- *Education.* A licensed real estate agent must maintain a certain number of hours of continuing education. Check to see if your agent is active with the local Realtor association, attends real estate conventions, and participates in extended education other than what is mandatory.
- *Reputation.* Get referrals. Does your Realtor have a favorable reputation? Every town will have Realtors with sterling (and shady!) characteristics.
- *Success.* Drive around your area. Do you see your Realtor's name on *For Sale* signs? What kind of neighborhoods are the signs posted in? Look on the office walls for performance awards.
- *Community involvement.* Does the Realtor participate in community activities? If so, he or she will have greater understanding of the "pulse" of the community, and much better attention to your specific needs. For instance, do you want to live in a neighborhood that has lots of children (or no children), social opportunities, privacy, or churches.

Once you settle on a Realtor, listen to her counsel. Keep something in mind, though: a seller's agent has a primary fiduciary responsibility to the person paying the commission (the seller). If you are a buyer, and the Realtor is acting as "dual agent" for buyer *and* seller, ask how that will affect negotiations.

How Do You Land the House of Your Dreams?

When you've found the perfect house (and have fallen in love with it and can't get it out of your mind), you want to make certain no one else beats you to the bargaining table. You want to hear those magic words "It's a deal!" as soon as possible. So as soon as you and the seller come to terms, a legal buy-sell contract is drafted. The buy-sell means you agree to buy the house from the seller, and the seller agrees to sell the house to only you, if all the terms of the buy-sell agreement are met. A buy-sell agreement almost always requires a deposit of money as a sign of "good faith." It can be as low as a few hundred dollars, or as high as a certain percentage of the selling price.

When drafting a buy-sell agreement, make sure you spell out *all* the terms of your agreement, no matter how small. For instance, if you are head-over-heels in love with the drapes, and you have been told they come with the house, make sure they are listed in the buy-sell: living room drapes to remain. **If you are buying the home, make sure you have a contingency plan or escape clause to release you if you can't obtain financing.** It's also important that you completely understand the contract you are signing, right down to your fiduciary responsibility to the real estate agent.

Your Realtor will apprise you of specifics, but when the actual transfer of title takes place, expect to pay (or participate in payment) for such things as transfer of titles, closing fees, drafting of documents, and title insurance. If you are selling a home, you will be responsible for the Realtor's fee. If a Realtor brings a qualified buyer, and at closing, or prior to closing, you back out, then you will probably owe a commission to the Realtor, who did exactly what you hired her to do. Your agreement with the Realtor is a binding agreement.

A good Realtor will help you assess your financial capabilities as a buyer and work with you so your bank or mortgage company can prequalify you financially. Realtors will also obtain comparable sales data to help you determine fair market value for the home you are buying or selling. Actually, obtaining a mortgage can be simplified by working with a Realtor. While securing a loan is not a Realtor's job, a good Realtor will help you brainstorm ideas for financing the mortgage for the home of your dreams. There are many options besides the conventional loans mentioned already. A good reference book is *Home Buyer's Confidential: The Insider's Guide to Buying Your Dream House, Condo, or Co-op,* by Maurice Dubois. Your bank or mortgage company might also be a good source for reference material.

What Kind of Loan Should You Apply For?

Most people get one of three types of loans when buying a home: FHA insured loans, VA guaranteed loans, and conventional loans.

1. *FHA.* An FHA "loan" is sometimes easier to obtain than conventional loans, because it is not so much a loan as it is an insurance policy against your defaulting. This "insurance policy" comes from the Federal Housing Authority. If a lender has to foreclose on property, it will be able to sell the home to the Department of Housing and Urban Development (HUD) or receive a percentage of the insurance amount until the loan can

be satisfied. Anyone can qualify for FHA who can qualify for conventional financing.

The FHA has several programs from which to choose, dependent upon such things as down payment, type of home you are purchasing, and amortization, which essentially means the specific period of time it will take to pay off the debt.

2. *VA.* The Department of Veteran's Affairs guarantees loans to veterans (and sometimes to husbands or wives of veterans). In a sense, this isn't a loan either, but a guarantee to the lender that the Veteran's Administration will back your loan if you default. The VA will generally purchase a house, rather than let a lender keep the foreclosed property.

3. *Conventional loans.* Conventional loans are most often used for mortgages over $100,000, since that is often the FHA limit. (FHA limits differ from region to region.) These are loans made by mortgage companies, banks, and savings and loans. Sometimes loans are insured by a mortgage insurance company to protect the lending institution if you default.

Keep in mind that you will probably pay "points" and origination fees. These are what lenders charge for their services when you obtain a loan. One point equals 1 percent of the cost of a loan. Every once in a while, the seller pays some of the points so the buyer can obtain financing. Points, and other closing costs, are based on percentages of the loan. Higher points usually mean lower interest; lower or no points usually mean higher interest. (Lenders have to get paid for loaning you money somehow, folks!) Obviously, if you plan to live in the home a long time, higher points and lower interest would be more favorable.

According to William Pivar, who has written more than thirty books on real estate, it's possible for home buyers to customize a mortgage loan to suit their needs.[1] Depending on your circumstances, certain loans may be more desirable than others. Some of Pivar's advice is adapted in the following paragraphs that list the ways you can customize your mortgage loan:

- If you are likely to be transferred, or move to a larger house in three to five years, consider a 5/25 loan. This loan offers a fixed rate that is about one percent lower than the thirty-year fixed rate. After five years, the loan is adjusted to one point *higher* than the current thirty-year rate. The advantage to you is the lower upfront rate.

- A 10/1 loan is the way to go if you know you will be making significantly more income after ten years. Under this loan, your interest is fixed for ten years at a lower rate than the thirty-year fixed rate. After ten years, the loan switches to a one-year ARM (Adjustable Rate Mortgage). ARM interest rates adjust according to predetermined factors, usually the prime interest rate or treasury bond rate.

- Fifteen-year fixed rate is the way to go if you plan to live in your home for at least twenty years. You get a slightly lower rate than the thirty-year fixed, and by paying your mortgage off in fifteen years, you save *tons* of money on interest.

- There are a couple of ways to look at a thirty-year mortgage. It is an option if you are stretching your pocketbook to buy your home. (As soon as financial circumstances change for the better, many people try to prepay their loans. Beware of prepayment penalties on some loans.)

On the other hand, if low interest rates are available, a thirty-year mortgage is a great way to go if your monthly payment is low, or if you might be able to invest in a 401(k) or similar investment, and make more than the interest you are paying on your mortgage. Of course, in a high interest environment, the opposite is true.

On What Criteria Do Lenders Base Their Decision?

Loan officers usually follow the 36 percent rule when determining your qualifications for a mortgage loan. In other words, once tallied, your projected mortgage payment, consumer debt, other loan payments, property taxes, and insurance must not exceed 36 percent of your gross income. (That leaves 64 percent for all your other expenses.) Lenders prefer that no more than 28 percent of the 36 percent goes toward the mortgage payment. For example: Suppose you made $2,000 gross each month. The amount of $720 (36 percent of $2,000) would be allowed for *all* indebtedness, of which $560 (28 percent) would be allowed for the mortgage. In other words, a lending institution will expect you to pay for all the above mentioned expenses, apart from the mortgage, with $160 each month.

Lenders also have specific qualifications for down payments. If you do not meet the down payment criteria, no loan. In cases where lending agencies accept less than 20 percent of the purchase price as your down payment, you will usually be required to purchase Mortgage Insurance Protection. MIP premiums are a percentage of the amount of the loan and are added to your monthly payment. If you must purchase MIP, check first with independent life insurance agents to compare costs, rather than automatically buy what the lender offers.

Should You Refinance Your Home?

Not all real estate transactions involve buying a home. It is becoming increasingly popular (and often significantly beneficial) to refinance your home. The refinancing of the home mortgage has become big business. Therefore, be a wise consumer if you are considering this option.

Conventional wisdom states that it is a good idea to refinance if the new interest rate is at least 2 percentage points lower than your current rate. It is not a good idea if you do not save much in interest, or if you will not stay in your home for at least two more years. (It takes that long to offset refinancing closing costs.)

You could save a lot of money and shorten the length of the refinanced loan if you continue to pay the original monthly mortgage payment.

What Is Your Attitude About Buying a Car?

After you have the house of your dreams, what are you planning to park in the garage? Is the old "beater" about ready to be retired?

Some people consider car payments a fact of life, and buy new cars regularly. Others regard car payments as a money trap, and keep "old faithful" on its tires as long as possible. Still others feel that since a car is necessary, they will do their best to cut costs in purchase, maintenance, and operation. This section is written with that position in mind.

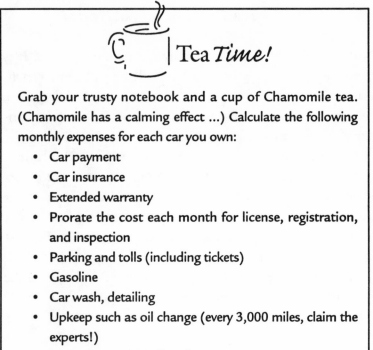

Tea *Time!*

Grab your trusty notebook and a cup of Chamomile tea. (Chamomile has a calming effect ...) Calculate the following monthly expenses for each car you own:

- Car payment
- Car insurance
- Extended warranty
- Prorate the cost each month for license, registration, and inspection
- Parking and tolls (including tickets)
- Gasoline
- Car wash, detailing
- Upkeep such as oil change (every 3,000 miles, claim the experts!)
- Maintenance, including tires

Should You Buy New or Used?

People who buy new cars do so for the advantages: warranty, safety, and lower interest incentives, to name a few. If you opt for new, and go to a dealership, you are likely to deal with more than one person: the salesman and his or her manager; the finance manager, who will try to sell you financing and a warranty; and in a big dealership, an accessories salesman who will try to get you to buy floor mats, molding, bumpers, undercoating, stereo, and more.

Caution: While there are times when dealers offer special low-interest rates that can't be beat, most likely you will be charged a higher interest rate if you finance your car loan (new or used) through the dealership. Wise consumers know this and will not let it happen. If you are considering the purchase of a car, shop for your own money, or ask if the dealer is charging additional interest. (Interest rates can be rather unpredictable.) Call some banks and credit unions to compare rates.

Logic tells us that buying a good used car is more sensible for the average person. There may be times, however, when you have to settle for a rattletrap because it is all you can afford. Keep a good attitude, and make it a goal to take steps toward affording something better next time. If possible, go without until that "affordable something better" comes along. That's what I did, and I was kind of sad when we gave my old beater away to a deserving college student. (I kind of liked the way everyone looked up when they heard my muffler-less car putt up the street.)

In our disposable, replace-everything society, many good used cars linger in car lots or are advertised in newspapers. When you buy used, your car does not depreciate as soon as you drive it away from the lot. (Depending on the make and model of the vehicle, a new car can reduce in value as much as $10,000 in the first year!) Also, used cars have lower license fees, sales tax, and (usually) lower insurance than new cars.

What Should You Know About Buying A Car?

When buying a car, it's wise to understand the following terms.

Rebate. A rebate is financial help from the factory, to help dealers move inventory—to "clear the lot." If you are considering a particular car, ask if a rebate will be offered soon or if the rebate terms will be improved in the near future.

Extended warranty. You will be asked if you want to purchase an extension on the warranty that comes with your car. Warranties usually cover a certain amount of time or a certain number of miles, depending on which comes first. For instance, you may buy a car with a five-year, 50,000-mile warranty. That means that the terms of the warranty will extend for as long as five years from purchase, or 50,000 miles, whichever happens first. So if you drive 50,000 miles in two years, you have used up your warranty.

An *extended* warranty is a hedge against the future cost of labor and parts. It is also a gamble: Will your car need a new engine or transmission beyond the factory guarantee? Will repair costs skyrocket? (If you bought an extended warranty and had to use it for a big-ticket item, you would certainly be glad!) Good arguments can be made for and against this extra cost. Extended warranties on newer models can be a good buy because of complicated electronics, which are nearly impossible to repair at home.

What else should you keep in mind when buying a car?

- Deal with someone who is reputable and honest.
- Decide ahead of time the make and model of car you would like.
- Research and establish the fair value of the car you want. Check with a trusted mechanic; shop many dealers; read books and magazines. Consult the famous "blue book" (found in your local library) for a general idea of value for that car.
- Buy quality and take good care of it, and it will last. Search for a car that has a reputation for dependability.
- Consider mileage and overall condition. Don't be afraid of high mileage when looking at a model that is well

known for trouble-free, high-mileage performance.

- Do not be unreasonable. The car dealer is in business to make a profit.
- Be a wise consumer. Ask the salesman for the *final cost* of the car. Many dealers will avoid telling you the purchase price of the car, and will stick to comments such as "Let's talk about what you can afford." Have you ever been to one of these places? The salesman writes a figure on a piece of paper, folds it, slides it across the table as if you were negotiating world peace, and makes his voice sound very serious as he says, "Can you handle this?" Baloney! All that does is make you think you are participating in the decision. Stop that silliness! Don't be a statistic.
- Be informed. Regrettably, women have helped perpetuate the myth that we know nothing about finances, or anything with moving parts! Do your homework. If you are dealing with a character who will not respect you as a customer, go elsewhere.
- Get help, if you need it. For a set fee, a nonprofit consumer organization called "CarBargains" claims it can get your new car at significant savings. You tell them what you want; they shop the package. Call and ask for their brochure. Ask directory assistance for their 1-800 number (1-800-555-1212).
- Before you buy, check with your car insurance agent about the premium for comprehensive and collision coverage on the car you are interested in. It is not uncommon for the cost of physical damage insurance on the new "used" car to be higher than that on the *newer* car it is replacing. For instance, if you replace a small, newer

compact with a slightly older luxury car, you will probably face higher insurance premiums.

- Save on insurance by buying your teens an older, but safe, car. Let them get their own sports car when they leave the nest. Opt for a four-door right now. Also, check into good student and driver training discounts.

Money and Thee: Finding Your Way

Buying a home or a car is a huge financial obligation. If you take time to inform yourself (this is one area where impulse shopping is verboten!) and then use your knowledge to your advantage, you will probably invest wisely. My counsel is the same that I gave to Jan in the first chapter. Do not become a slave to the mortgage payment or to car payments. Live happily in your little castle; drive a safe and sensible car; and by all means, live *within* your means. The next—and last—chapter will help you to do just that.

Now it's your turn to write. Think about the chapter you have just read. How does it apply to you? Soul-search a little, and jot down your thoughts.

Where I am now: _____

_____

_____

Where I'd like to be: _____

_____

_____

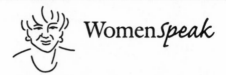 Women*Speak*

"Tenth anniversaries are supposed to be special occasions. Instead, ours was spent listening to a sales pitch on why we should join a 'consumer's club.' My husband had a reputation for being an easy catch on the phone, so he was lured to a 'special presentation' with the promise of great savings. Unwillingly, I went along with the plan. Many others turned up to learn all about group buying power.

"The catch (and first red flag) was that, unlike the current warehouse clubs with annual membership fees of $30-$35, this club required a membership fee of $850, spread over three installments. After that you paid yearly renewal fees of $150. As a member you could order everything from cars to furniture to appliances, and on and on. (Everything was ordered out of one of their many catalogs—no stock was on hand.)

"The second red flag appeared when we were told we had to make a decision that night—no going home to sleep on the proposal. I wanted to walk away, but my husband thought it would be a good idea. Reluctantly, I was talked into it.

"Over the first year we bought only a microwave and several pairs of pantyhose. We never bought a car through them, since the make we decided on was not available through their club. When renewal time came around, I was able to convince my husband it was time to cut our losses and get out.

"The moral? Learn to pay attention to those red flags. If something doesn't seem right, don't do it. If you're being pressured, walk away."

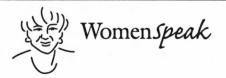 Women*Speak*

"How I wish I knew when I was young what I know now about money management ... [For example] not using packaged ingredients instead of fresh ones. It costs more and doesn't really save any time in the end."

———

"We [husband and wife] have fun together. Although it's extremely important to save and invest, it's not smart to make yourselves miserable. Go out to eat when the fridge is empty and you've had a long week. Or stay home, make pizza (together of course!) with whatever's left in the fridge, rent a movie (walk to the movie store together and talk about your favorite movies), and then be couch potatoes the rest of the night. Or eat at home and walk to the ice cream store. Look at the beautiful houses on the way and dream expensive dreams. Won't cost you a penny, and you'll burn calories to boot!"

twelve

Eating and Dressing Within Your Means

This chapter is dedicated to helping you with spending decisions in two categories—food and clothing—and offers tips and suggestions about wise spending practices that can be applied to just about any other category.

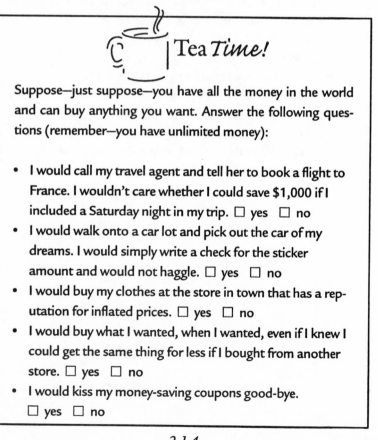

Tea *Time!*

Suppose—just suppose—you have all the money in the world and can buy anything you want. Answer the following questions (remember—you have unlimited money):

- I would call my travel agent and tell her to book a flight to France. I wouldn't care whether I could save $1,000 if I included a Saturday night in my trip. ☐ yes ☐ no
- I would walk onto a car lot and pick out the car of my dreams. I would simply write a check for the sticker amount and would not haggle. ☐ yes ☐ no
- I would buy my clothes at the store in town that has a reputation for inflated prices. ☐ yes ☐ no
- I would buy what I wanted, when I wanted, even if I knew I could get the same thing for less if I bought from another store. ☐ yes ☐ no
- I would kiss my money-saving coupons good-bye.
  ☐ yes ☐ no

What Should You Know About Buying Food?

Chances are, many of you surprised yourselves with answers to the above Tea *Time*. Know why? Because many of you have already developed frugal habits and will not recklessly spend your money, no matter how much you have, because being frugal means being smart. It means having a general idea about the price of something, so you can spot a good deal. It means not purchasing on impulse. It also means allowing yourself the freedom to purchase on impulse from time to time! It means buying quality so you only buy once. It means taking care of what you have. It means sharing with others every time you can.

This is the truth: I only spend $100 each month on groceries for my husband and me. I do so by observing some basic rules.

1. *Eat seasonally.* We adjusted our eating habits to what is currently in season, and we save overall. Strawberries and asparagus should be enjoyed during early summer months (or frozen for winter use); apples should be a staple of your diet in the fall; hard squashes should simmer in winter stews. Meat has its season, too, and demand for certain cuts brings prices *up*. Anything destined for the grill will inflate in price during barbecue season; heavier cuts such as roasts begin to soar when the first frost hits.

2. *Stock up on seasonal bargains and loss leaders.* Baking supplies are usually slashed in price during Thanksgiving and Christmas holidays. Picnic supplies drop in price in June. Stores will offer special deals on hams at Easter, corned beef in March. Stock up when prices are attractive.

3. *Don't waste!* No sense cutting a great deal on lettuce if it rots in the fridge. There are times when something gets old before its time and sounds the green goop alert. It happens to us all. Try to store food wisely, and use it before it goes to waste.

4. *Use coupons—sometimes!* No sense in buying something with a coupon if it is not something you would normally buy. That means you will tote it home, and it will just sit in your cupboard and occupy space. Learn to use coupons wisely. I am reminded of a seminar I gave once, on frugal living. I walked from table to table and asked each group of women to give me a dime. Then I walked to a door, opened it, and flung the dimes as far into the parking lot as I could. "That, ladies," I announced to the flabbergasted group, "is what you are doing if you do not use a coupon for something you would normally buy." (Yes, I did see at least one woman scouring the parking lot later in the day.)

5. *Use what you have.* Most of us could feed our family for weeks by using what we've amassed in the cupboards and freezer.

6. *Buy in bulk.* Any time you pay a store to package or process something for you, you pay more. I rarely buy individual servings of anything, and that includes pop or juice. (I don't see the sense in paying lots more for convenience, if I determine that the convenience I paid for simply means not needing to take one extra minute to chop something in my own kitchen.) If something is in danger of decay, I will freeze it, if possible (a great thing to do with bananas and lemons), or I will incorporate it into the next meal and try to cook extra servings to be frozen for later use, or for Joe's lunch pail.

7. *Learn how to cook.* I believe the main factor in successfully maintaining a low food budget is **knowing how to cook**. I have a few standby recipes, yet we have such a variety of assorted beans, pasta, and rice in our pantry that we seldom eat the same recipe twice. Meat makes occasional appearances on our table and is often used sparingly, more as an ingredient than the main course.

A FEW FOOD SHOPPING TIPS

- Shop with a list; stick to the list. Leave two spaces blank for loss leaders or an occasional impulse item.
- Buy only what your family will eat. Don't shop when you are hungry; it's true that you will buy more! Leave the kids at home. (Ever notice those cute little shopping carts for the under-five set? Good training [to become an out-of-control shopper].)
- Eye-level products are often more expensive. Better for you to bend and reach, anyway.
- Most stores will break up bunches of produce to sell you a smaller amount.
- Try to use a coupon when the item is also on sale. Double whammy.
- Buy spices and herbs in bulk from the health food store or bulk food store. Buy small quantities because, over time, spices lose their strength.
- Stay clear of name-brand boxed cereals, if you can. Buy generic or make oatmeal. Cereal is one of the most expensive aisles in the grocery store!
- Buy generic or store brands, unless you are really stuck on a particular product.
- Know your prices! If you do better at a warehouse store, shop there. Don't hoard, though. Buy as much as you need in the foreseeable future, unless you are vulnerable to natural disaster. (Toilet paper will always be on sale!)
- Never buy a dairy product without checking the expiration date.

Tea *Time!*

Should shopping be fun? Yes! Absolutely!
Should shopping be FOR fun? No! Absolutely not!

Food takes a big chunk out of our budgets, that's for sure, but if we develop certain skills in purchasing, and in the kitchen, we can significantly reduce the amount we spend. What happens when we develop these skills? *They become routine. Automatic. Second nature. No big deal.*

Clothing, now, that's another thing entirely! I mean, we don't want to wear *last year's styles,* do we?

What Should You Know About Buying Clothes?

Once you learn the simple trick of following the "retail dateline," you will be up to your buttons in *haute couture!* Here is how it works.

Nearly all stores must clear out inventory when the next "season" rolls around, be it Christmas, summer, or back-to-school. In order to sell off inventory, clearance or out-of-stock sales are offered at drastically reduced prices, since hardly any stores send inventory back to the warehouse. Winter and fall clothing should begin to be cleared out around the end of January. This is an excellent time to buy a dynamite sweater for someone's upcoming birthday. Start watching for spring closeouts around the last week in April.

Summer clothing should begin to be cleared out around the

middle to end of July, as many stores try to be 100 percent back-to-school by then. Certainly, by the end of summer, there will be spectacular buys on lightweight clothing. How about buying a cotton skirt to tuck away as a Christmas present? Most fall and back-to-school clothing will close out around the end of October.

The best sales are usually clearance sales, which start at 30 percent off. (Just about every piece of clothing in a store will sport a 25 percent markdown at one time or another.) "Red tag" is another thing to look for; it means the item has been marked down drastically. There are such things as "pre-season" sales, as well. These usually top off at 25 percent markdowns on clothes for the upcoming season—often as much as three months before the season begins! The bonus to pre-season buying is that there is more of a selection to choose from early in the season.

Tea *Time!*

Walk over to your closet right now. Go ahead, I'll wait. Now, what do you see? Blouses and skirts and sweaters and vests and pants and dresses and shoes ... that you hardly ever wear. Am I right? We are all guilty of Bulging Closet Syndrome.

Prune your closet. Get rid of anything you do not wear. Someone else might need it. Keep classic styles that are attractive on you and sport the right color for your complexion. Then don't buy anything unless it will blend with what you already have.

A FEW BUYING TIPS

Try these tips on "for size" and see if it "shrinks" your clothing budget (authors get giddy when they near the completion of a book).

- Merchandise is normally displayed thirty days before it is put on sale.

- "Clean-up-in-season" is a sacred phrase in retail. It means items with a seasonal application must be sold during that season or holiday time. For instance, consider Valentine's Day, the most costly day for retail stores. It is hard to buy inventory for this holiday. What's a merchant to do with two dozen heart-shaped boxes of candy—on February 15? A good department store will be out of seasonal merchandise at the peak of the season. If you wait until "out of stock" price slashing, the nice selection will be long gone. However, retailers reduce prices dramatically on goods that have lingered beyond the peak selling period.

- Think "timeless," not "dated." No matter where you buy clothes, opt for timeless, classic styles that will survive each new season's fashion industry assault. For example, one necessary outfit is a great-fitting pair of slacks or a skirt, crisp white blouse, and blazer.

- After you study your closet, make a list of necessities to complete your mix and match (and classic!) wardrobe.

- If you are patient, trips with your list to the mall (to several department stores) during any of the projected out-of-stock sales will probably net you a terrific buy. This is always a great opportunity to buy Christmas or birthday gifts at significant savings.

- Learn to accessorize and use color to your advantage. Add good posture, a confident gait, a look-someone-in-the-eye smile, and you will dazzle us all!
- Always factor in your cleaning bills. Clothes that require special cleaning can cost up to three times as much, overall. Three fabrics that almost always need dry-cleaning: rayon, wool, and acetate. (If you must dry-clean, use a dry cleaner that charges on a per-pound basis, and cleans his dry-cleaning fluid regularly!)
- "Specials" are usually sales for items seldom or never carried before. Often a "this ad only" kind of offer, and usually loss leaders, they represent a special deal the retailer got from a manufacturer. Traditionally, the quality is poorer than normal merchandise.
- Avoid high traffic areas stocked with impulse items! This merchandise has the highest markup and is usually the "in" fashion. Best sales are found in the back of the department.

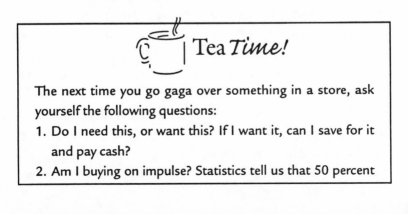

Tea *Time!*

The next time you go gaga over something in a store, ask yourself the following questions:

1. Do I need this, or want this? If I want it, can I save for it and pay cash?
2. Am I buying on impulse? Statistics tell us that 50 percent

---

of what we buy is on impulse, and 25 percent of what we buy we don't need.

3. Am I using my credit card? Use of a credit card weakens resistance. According to Consumer Credit Counseling Service, many stores want customers to use credit, because research shows they spend nearly twice as much as cash-paying customers.

4. Can I use savings? If so, would a loan from savings wipe out my emergency fund?

5. Can I buy this product on lay-away and make monthly payments?

6. Can I wait and buy this item at a seasonal sale?

Most of us spend a lot of money buying things we don't need. If we would simply stop and ask these kinds of questions before we buy, we would be not only wiser, but richer!

It's a woman thing to want to wear fashion and to look pretty. And we should. And we can. If we manage our resources wisely, learn a few basics about colors, styles, and quality, and practice sensible consumer tips, we can dazzle everyone we meet! Like everything else in this book, it takes a little practice, a little motivation, and a whole lot of the right attitude. There is no reason you can't achieve the kind of financial security and freedom that allows for a shopping spree at the mall every now and then.

There are books galore that offer tips on thrifty living, and nary a magazine is published that doesn't have its say when it comes to saving our shekels, whether we're going to the grocery store or gas pump. Invest in a book that suits your style; some are strong toward "homemade," some emphasize simple living, some are stringent, some are loaded with helpful hints for the harried twenty-first-century woman. When you purchase your book, give it a place of prominence on your nightstand, or next to the tub. Turn to it often, as you would a manual. Each author is practiced at the art of frugal living and wants to ease your financial struggle. If I may be so bold, I recommend my book *1,001 Bright Ideas to Stretch Your Dollars.*[1]

Money and Thee: Finding Your Way

It is cold and black outside. There is just enough light from our living room window to illuminate some of the outside darkness. As I look up from my computer screen and peer out my office window, I see clear contrast: dark and light. That is a good analogy for this book. There are times in every woman's life—whether it is because of relationships, health, or finances—that her path, once dark, becomes illuminated. Her stumbling lessens as her steps become more certain, and she now has light to guide her. My prayer is that this book has shed some light on your path, my sister. At least enough light to keep you from tripping again, or to help you find your way back up if you fall. My greatest prayer is that you will invite the true Light of the world, Jesus Christ, to hold your hand as you walk that path, and that he will fill your heart with his perfect peace.

This is your last time to write. Think about what you have just read in this chapter. Think back over this whole book. How does it apply to you? Soul-search a little, and jot down your thoughts.

Where I am now: _____

_____

_____

Where I'd like to be: _____

_____

_____

Soli Deo Gloria

Appendix A

A Word About Health Insurance

Financing health care is a major concern to many women, if not most women. Until the health insurance industry develops sound and affordable policies, it is utterly critical that each one of us stays up-to-date with our policies and reviews the coverage of our health insurance at least yearly. Congress has attempted to narrow the gaps for people who suffer with expensive health care, but it is still necessary to offer some pointers:

- Under certain conditions, you can withdraw funds from your IRA, without penalty, for medical expenses. If you deduct medical expenses from your federal tax return, those costs that exceed 7.5 percent of your gross adjusted income can be funded from your IRA. Also, if you are unemployed for at least twelve weeks, you can withdraw from your IRA for health insurance premiums. Although you aren't penalized for premature withdrawal, the money will be subject to tax.

- Small businesses (fifty or fewer employees) and those who are self-employed can set up a Medical Savings Account, which is linked to high-deductible catastrophic health insurance. The self-employed can deduct 100 percent of contributions to an MSA, which are tax and penalty-free when withdrawn for IRS-defined medical expenses. At this writing, an MSA is in a somewhat experimental stage.

- "Preexisting conditions" clauses are becoming limited or prohibited by law. After twelve months of coverage, no preexisting condition limit can be imposed on people who maintain their coverage, even if they change jobs or plans. Neither can a group discriminate against an employee or dependent based on health status.

- The COBRA law provides that if you leave your job, you can remain in your group health plan—at your expense—for up to eighteen months (three years if you become widowed or divorced).

Health Insurance Choices

Fee for service. This was just about the only way things were once done: pay a deductible and see anyone you wish for medical care; the company will pay a percentage of "allowable" costs, and you pay the rest. This is an expensive option, especially when your health insurance company considers that last visit to your chiropractor not at all usual, customary, and reasonable!

Managed care. Under this type of plan, you pay a yearly or monthly premium and, theoretically, never see a doctor's bill again. This is because you use a specified network of contracted medical care establishments that are offered by the health plan. You may pay a nominal copayment for each office visit. This particular option stresses preventive medicine.

Health Maintenance Organization. This is essentially a managed care plan with just about all medical services provided at a central location, where you must go for services.

Preferred Provider Organization. This is another variation of the managed care program, but it allows you to see any doctor or specialist you choose—as long as you choose from a list provided by your insurer. Under a PPO you will typically pay 10 percent to 20 percent of the bill.

Appendix B

Protecting Your Legacy:
Helping Your Parents With Their Estate Plan

M any of us face the bewildering task of caring for our senior parents. Hard enough to juggle emotions with the reality of physical and custodial care, but what to do about Mom's or Dad's dwindling bank account? In particular, nursing home costs are eating away at everything.

At this writing, your parents can still protect a portion of their savings from overwhelming long-term health costs, through Medicaid. Specifically, the law now allows parents to give a portion of their savings to children (or others). By giving away money, your parents might reduce assets enough to become eligible for Medicaid.

- Medicaid rules allow your parents to protect "exempt" assets (home, household goods, car, prepaid funeral). *Caution:* Check with the state your parents reside in for its rules.
- Medicaid allows the creation of specialized trusts to preserve assets.
- Medicaid allows you to purchase a Medicaid annuity or promissory note, which will help keep parents financially secure when one of them enters a nursing home.
- Medicare or Medicaid may pay for home-health care and delay (or offset) the need for nursing-home care.

If your parents are no longer capable of making wise, responsible financial decisions, talk with them about a custodial trust account.

Custodial Trust Account

These accounts can be established with most banks. Under this arrangement, the person in control of the money in the account is not the person who owns the money. Examples would include parents who oversee an account for a minor child, or an adult child, or friend, who manages an account on behalf of an elderly person. However, because there is little to no accountability, unless there is an audit, or unless the custodian is court-appointed, be aware that this responsibility can be abused.

Notes

One
1. Dahlstrom & Co., *Out of Hock* (Halliston, Mass.: Dahlstrom, 1993).

Two
1. Jerry and Ramona Tuma and Tim LaHaye, *Smart Money* (Sisters, Ore.: Multnomah, 1994), 143.
2. Karen O'Connor, *When Spending Takes the Place of Feeling* (Nashville: Thomas Nelson, 1992), 73.

Three
1. Ron Blue, *Mastering Money in Your Marriage* (Ventura, Calif.: Regal, 1993), 9.
2. Walter Martin, *Tithing: Is It New Testament?* (San Juan Capistrano, Calif.: Christian Research Institute, 1980).
3. Stephanie Bullock, "Oseola McCarty Changed My Life," *Family Circle*, April 22, 1997, 52, 54.

Five
1. James L. Paris and J.W. Dicks, *Financial CPR* (Orlando, Fla: Creation House, 1993), 121.

Six
1. Susan Forward and Craig Buck, *Money Demons* (New York: Bantam, 1994), 2.
2. Forward and Buck, 222.

Seven
1. Bullock, 54.
2. Sherman S. Smith, *Put Your Money Where Your Heart Is* (Chicago: Meister, 1996), 34.
3. Kathryn Shaw, *Investment Clubs: A Low Cost Education in the Stock Market* (Williamsburg, Va.: Lake Shore, 1992), 9.

Eight
1. Daniel D. Busby, Kent E. Barber, and Robert L. Temple, "Worry-Free Money Management," *Christian American*, January/February 1997, 40–42.

2. Smith, 122.

Nine

1. R.K. Harrison, general ed., *Encyclopedia of Biblical and Christian Ethics* (Nashville: Thomas Nelson, 1992), 115.
2. Maggie Mahar, "Splitsville," *Barron's,* June 23, 1997, 31.
3. Mahar, 31.
4. Forward and Buck, 23.
5. Margorie L. Engel and Diana D. Gould, *The Divorce Decision Workbook* (New York: McGraw-Hill, 1992), 47.

Ten

1. Smith, 157.

Eleven

1. Maurice Dubois, *Home Buyer's Confidential* (New York: McGraw-Hill, 1991).
2. William Pivar, "The Best Mortgages for Different Stages in Life," *Bottom Line,* July 15, 1997, 6.

Twelve

1. Cynthia G. Yates, *1,001 Bright Ideas to Stretch Your Dollars* (Ann Arbor, Mich.: Servant, 1995).

Bibliography

I wish to acknowledge the following authors, experts, and organizations. This book is, in part, a result of the wisdom and counsel offered through these books, articles, newsletters, radio programs, and tapes.

American Association of Retired Persons. "Living Trusts Scams and Older Consumers."

Barrett, Bill. *For Sale By Owner*. video tape. *Marketology*, Bill Barrett.

Blue, Ron. *Mastering Money in Your Marriage*. Ventura, Calif.: Regal, 1993.

— *Taming the Money Monster*. Colorado Springs: Focus on the Family, 1989.

Bullock, Stephanie. "Oseola McCarty Changed My Life." *Family Circle*, April 22, 1997.

Burkett, Larry. *Money Matters*. A radio program. Gainesville, Fla.: Christian Financial Concepts, current & daily.

— *Women Leaving the Workplace*. Chicago: Moody, 1995.

Busby, Daniel D., Kent E. Barber, and Robert L. Temple. "Worry-Free Money Management." *Christian American*, January/February 1997.

Clapp, Rodney. "Why the Devil Takes Visa." *Christianity Today*, October 7, 1996.

Dahlstrom & Co. *Out Of Hock*. Halliston, Mass.: Dahlstrom & Co., 1993.

Dubois, Maurice. *Home Buyer's Confidential: The Insider's Guide to Buying Your Dream House, Condo, or Co-op*. New York: McGraw-Hill, 1991.

Dunton, Loren, and Kim Ciccarelli Banta. *Preserving Family Wealth and Peace of Mind*. Chicago: Probus, 1994.

Elwell, Walter A., ed. *Evangelical Commentary on the Bible*. Grand Rapids, Mich.: Baker, 1989.

Engel, Margorie L., and Diana D. Gould. *The Divorce Decision Workbook*. New York: McGraw-Hill, 1992.

Forward, Susan, and Craig Buck. *Money Demons*. New York: Bantam, 1994.

Gaudio, Peter E., and Virginia S. Nicols. *Your Retirement Benefits*. New York: John Wiley & Sons, 1992.

Hamon, Edward A. *How to Write Your Own Premarital Agreement*. Clearwater, Fla.: Sphinx, 1993.

Harris, Marlys. "Smart Ways to Save Money." *Family Life*, Winter 96/97.

Harrison, R.K., ed. *Encyclopedia of Biblical and Christian Ethics.* Nashville: Thomas Nelson, 1992.

Holzman, Robert S. *Encyclopedia of Estate Planning.* Greenwich, Conn.: Boardroom Classics, 1997.

Kaye, Steven D. "A Plastic-Poisoned Retirement." *U.S. News and World Report,* November 4, 1996.

Mahar, Maggie. "Splitsville." *Barron's,* June 23, 1997.

Martin, Don, and Renee Martin. *Family Survival Kit: How to Avoid Financial Chaos.* New York: Villard Books, 1988.

Martin, Walter. *Tithing: Is It New Testament?* San Juan Capistrano, Calif.: Christian Research Institute, 1980.

McKibben, Bill. "Christmas Unplugged." *Christianity Today,* December 9, 1996.

O'Connor, Karen. *When Spending Takes the Place of Feeling.* Nashville: Thomas Nelson, 1992.

Paris, James L., and J.W. Dicks. *Financial CPR.* Orlando, Fla.: Creation House, 1993.

Pivar, William. "The Best Mortgages for Different Stages in Life." *Bottom Line,* July 15, 1997.

Quinn, Jane Bryant. "Investment Clubs: What Makes Them Work?" *Good Housekeeping,* September 1997.

Quint, Barbara Gilder. "The New Deal From Uncle Sam." *Family Circle,* August 5, 1997.

Schlayer, Mary Elizabeth, and Marilyn H. Cooley. *How to Be a Financially Secure Woman.* New York: Rawson Associates, 1978.

Shaw, Kathryn. *Investment Clubs: A Low Cost Education in the Stock Market.* Williamsburg, Va.: Lake Shore, 1992.

Smith, Sherman S. *Exploding the Doomsday Money Myths.* Nashville: Thomas Nelson, 1994.

— *Put Your Money Where Your Heart Is.* Chicago: Meister, 1996.

Stern, Linda. "Get Credit Where It's Due." *Modern Maturity,* September-October 1997.

Tannenbaum, Barbara. "The Language of Health Care." *Best Years,* 1997.

Tuma, Jerry, Ramona Tuma and Tim LaHaye. *Smart Money.* Sisters, Ore.: Multnomah, 1994.

Yates, Cynthia G. *1,001 Bright Ideas to Stretch Your Dollars.* Ann Arbor, Mich.: Servant, 1995.

Index

Other Books by Cynthia G. Yates

1,001 Bright Ideas to Stretch Your Dollars
Pinch Your Pennies, Hoard Your Quarters,
and Collar Your Dollars

Cynthia Yates incorporates "Ten Commandments of Thrifty Living" into every aspect of daily life: food preparation and storage, hospitality, gift-giving, car and home purchase and maintenance, home decorating, and much more. Readers will be challenged both financially and spiritually to use their resources to bring glory to God. *$10.99*

The Complete Guide to Creative Gift Giving

The perfect book for anyone who wants to know how to give creative, meaningful gifts, *The Complete Guide to Creative Gift Giving* suggests gifts the recipients will never forget. It offers ideas for every gift-giving reason and season—not just Christmas and birthdays—emphasizing gifts that have long-lasting value, that are creative, enjoyable, and fun to receive. *$10.99*